CW01091312

THE
MENTAL HEALTH ACT
COMMISSION

FOURTH
BIENNIAL REPORT
1989-1991

*Laid before Parliament by the
Secretary of State for Health
pursuant to Section 121 (10) of the
Mental Health Act 1983*

DECEMBER 1991

London: HMSO

CONTENTS

Part IV. Other Commission Activities

CHAIRMAN'S FOREWORD

While members of the Commission continued largely undisturbed throughout the period of this report to visit hospital and respond to patients complaints, the preponderant aspect of Commission life was a centralising of its administration in new officers in Nottingham. The period immediately preceding the transfer saw the departure of the Commission's Secretary, Mr Graham Howard, who served the Commission well for four years, latterly during the transitional and disrupting phase between the decision to alter the structure of the Commission's operations only six years after its statutory creation and its implementation. He has been appointed Manager of the Mental Health Unit at Fulbourn Hospital near Cambridge. The Commission wishes him well.

The Commission's Chief Executive took up his post in early 1990, some time after Mr Howard's departure. The gap was filled by Mrs Elizabeth Parker, a principal in the Department of Health who had earlier experience of Mental Health Administration as the Director of the Special Hospitals Research Unit and subsequently in the division of the Department of Health, which has the responsibility for among other things, the Commission. She came in November 1989 as acting Secretary to the Commission to supervise the closure of three regional offices and to install the new centralised administration (only three out of seventeen members of staff remained with the Commission after the move to Nottingham). That the operation was achieved with a minimal amount of disruption is attributable in no small measure to her administration and management skills. Her return in September 1990 to the Department of Health, to head the unit dealing with community care for the mentally ill, at least meant that her contact with the Commission was not totally lost. The Commission will remain indebted to Mrs Parker for her part in re-establishing the Commission in its revised framework.

Much of the credit for the ease with which the Commission settled into its new Head Quarters is due to the staff, who for the second half of this period have worked with admirable efficiency, all but three of them having had little or no experience of working for a unique body of 90 part-time professionals acting as watch-dogs over the rights and interests of detained patients in the mental health system. They have exhibited great patience while a long overdue computerised system is being installed. Their workload has been heavier than they were entitled to expect since the staffing levels were calculated other than on the basis of a manual system of administration. The staff have cheerfully met the requirements of often demanding members of the Commission, who have every reason to be be grateful for the service provided, given the novelty of the tasks set for staff.

The composition of the Commission membership has changed significantly. About a third of the members completed their period of office in the Autumn of 1989. With very few exceptions this meant that none of the original members who appointed in September 1983, when the Commission began its life, remained on the Commission. It is a tribute to the dedication and work of all the original members that the Commission stands in such good stead today.

When the Commission began the daunting task of visiting NHS hospitals and the Special Hospitals there was no guidance of experience to hand. The Commission had to find its own way forward and establish its credibility with the public and with those working in the mental health field. The pattern of operational activities adopted by the Commission in the early years has done much to enhance and improve the protection and safeguards of the interests of detained patients.

The Commission has operated with a high degree of autonomy as a result of Ministerial desire to let the Commission perform its role within the mental health system without governmental interference. The period under review has been characterised by no less autonomy for the Commission, but with more helpful contact with Ministers. The current Parliamentary Under Secretary of State for Health, Mr Stephen Dorrell, MP, has given constant encouragement to the Commission by his evident interest in the Commission's work and the forthcoming manner in which Commission issues have been treated in meetings with him.

Parliamentary approval in January 1990 of the Secretary of State's Code of Practice has meant the first extension of the Commission's functions delegated to it by the Secretary of State. The monitoring of the Code has been devolved on the Commission, and it will be reporting to the Secretary of State on the first two years of the Code's application by those working within the Mental Health system towards the end of 1991.

The last two years provide for me a stark contrast to the earlier two years of my chairmanship. My initiation in 1987 into the workings of the Commission was undeniably difficult. The regional structure had created a diffusion in policy and practice (which I found unhelpful for a body that was set up by statute as a national watchdog for detained patients), and not a number of bloodhounds snapping at the heels of divided parts of England and Wales. The Commission is now centralised and is a more cohesive and a more effective multi-disciplinary body. For that to have been achieved I have to thank, with warmth and respect, the members of the Commission.

Louis Blom-Cooper QC

Members of the Mental Health Act Commission 1989-91

Mr L Blom-Cooper QC — Chairman
Professor E Murphy — Vice Chairman

Ms A Aiyegbusi
Mr J R Allam
Mr P Allott*
Dr J B Ashcroft
Mr A G Ball
Dr M Barnes
Mr A Barsted*
Mrs V Bellau
Mrs C J Bennett
Mrs O J Benyon*
Mr D A Black
Dr A J Blowers
Ms C Bollinger*
Mr J M Bowyer
Mrs S L Breach
Dr O Briscoe*
Dr A Broadhurst
Mr E Bromley*
Mr P Brotherhood
Mr M B Brown
Mr J Bury*
Mr G Bye
Mrs S H Cawthra*
Mr E A R Chitty
Dr R Cope*
Miss P Cushing
Mr A R Dabbs
Dr K A Day
Ms J Deeley
Professor B Dimond
Dr R Dolan
Dr D L F Dunleavy
Mr T Eager*
Mr M Edwards-Evans*
Mrs P G S Entwistle
Dr M Evans*
Mr P W H Fennell*
Dr S Fernando
Mr J D Finch
Mrs J Forman-Hardy
Mrs R M F Fraser
Mr R K Gardner*
Dr D Gasper
Dr H Ghadiali

Dr N L Gittleson
Mrs C Goonatillake*
Dr E B Gordon
Mr M J Graham*
Mr J Graham-White*
Dr J S Grimshaw*
Mr M J Gunn
Dr K Hamadah
Mrs J B Hanham*
Dr M A Harper
Dr P Harper — deceased
Dr A Hauck
Canon A J Hawes
Dr P Hettiaratchy
Dr D Hide
Dr E Howarth*
Mr P Hughes*
Dr J Hurst*
Dr P M Jeffreys*
Mrs T Jowell*
Mr G Lakes
Mrs E A Land*
Dr G E Langley*
Mrs S Lee
Mr G D Lees*
Mrs A R M Lewis*
Mr B R Lillington*
Mr R C Lingham
Miss G Linton
Mrs V Lipscomb
Mrs C Llewelyn-Jones
Mr H McClarron
Dr M T Malcolm
Mr S S Manikon
Mrs L Mason
Mrs M Meacher
Dr I H Mian
Mrs I Midforth
Mr A Milligan
Mrs M R Morris*
Mr S A R Mumford
Mr T M Napier
Dr C Neal
Miss I Nutting

Mrs E Owen
Dr F Oyebode
Mr J Palacios*
Mr A Parkin
Mr D Parkin*
Mr T Peel*
Mrs M Phillips
Dr R M Philpott
Mr J M Pinschof*
Mr H A Prins*
Dr I G Pryce
Dr Y J Rao
Mrs E Rassaby
Ms G Richardson
Mrs M R Roberts
Dr M Rowton-Lee
Mrs A Samuels
Mrs A Scott-Fordham*
Ms L Scott-Moncreiff
Dr N P Seberatnam
Mrs C Selim
Mr J Sharich
Ms L Sinclair
Mr B Smith
Mr G Smith*
Ms P Spinks
Mr R Stables
Mrs B J Stroll
Mr M B Taylor
Mr H A Teaney
Mr B G J Thorne
Mr R M Timson*
Mr D Torpy
Mrs S E Turner*
Mr H Vickers
Mr A Watson
Mr C N S Watts*
Professor D West
Mr L J Wilson
Mr R J Wix
Professor A J Yeates
Dr A S Zigmond

*Denotes retired members.

9

MENTAL HEALTH ACT COMMISSION — STAFFING AT 30.6.91

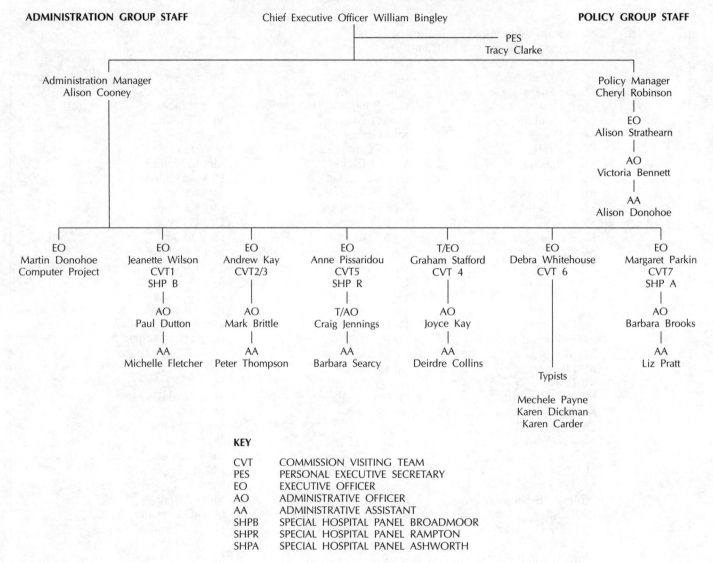

ADMINISTRATION GROUP STAFF

Chief Executive Officer William Bingley

POLICY GROUP STAFF

PES
Tracy Clarke

Administration Manager
Alison Cooney

Policy Manager
Cheryl Robinson

EO
Alison Strathearn

AO
Victoria Bennett

AA
Alison Donohoe

EO	EO	EO	EO	T/EO	EO	EO
Martin Donohoe	Jeanette Wilson	Andrew Kay	Anne Pissaridou	Graham Stafford	Debra Whitehouse	Margaret Parkin
Computer Project	CVT1	CVT2/3	CVT5	CVT 4	CVT 6	CVT7
	SHP B		SHP R			SHP A
	AO	AO	T/AO	AO		AO
	Paul Dutton	Mark Brittle	Craig Jennings	Joyce Kay		Barbara Brooks
	AA	AA	AA	AA		AA
	Michelle Fletcher	Peter Thompson	Barbara Searcy	Deirdre Collins		Liz Pratt

Typists

Mechele Payne
Karen Dickman
Karen Carder

KEY

CVT	COMMISSION VISITING TEAM
PES	PERSONAL EXECUTIVE SECRETARY
EO	EXECUTIVE OFFICER
AO	ADMINISTRATIVE OFFICER
AA	ADMINISTRATIVE ASSISTANT
SHPB	SPECIAL HOSPITAL PANEL BROADMOOR
SHPR	SPECIAL HOSPITAL PANEL RAMPTON
SHPA	SPECIAL HOSPITAL PANEL ASHWORTH

1.
THE FUNCTIONS OF THE COMMISSION

The Mental Health Act Commission (MHAC) is a Special Health Authority and was established in 1983. It consists of some ninety part-time members, including lay persons, lawyers, doctors, nurses, social workers, psychologists and other specialists (see page iii for list of members). It has a Chairman and Vice Chairman and is staffed by Civil Servants seconded from the Department of Health.

The functions of the MHAC are:

a. To keep under review the operation of the Mental Health Act 1983 in respect of patients detained under the Act or patients liable to be detained under the Act.

b. To visit and interview in private patients detained under the Act in hospitals and mental nursing homes.

c. To investigate complaints which fall within the Commission's remit.

d. To review decisions to withhold the mail of patients detained in the Special Hospitals.

e. To appoint medical practitioners and others to give second opinions in cases where this is required by the Act.

f. To monitor the implementation of the Code of Practice and advise Ministers on amendments.

g. To publish a biennial report.

h. To offer advice to Ministers on matters falling within the Commission's remit.

Appendix 1 contains relevant extracts from the Mental Health Act concerning the Commission and the relevant statutory instruments.

Reports about the undertaking of these responsibilities will be found in later chapters.

2.
THE COMMISSION'S NEW STRUCTURE

2.1 Introduction

In 1989 the Secretary of State for Health accepted the main recommendations of a review of Commission activities, carried out by the Commission itself with the assistance of the Department of Health. The major consequence has been the end of the Commission's regional structure (see the Commission's Third Biennial Report), the closure of its offices in London and Liverpool, the establishment of a central administration in Nottingham and the creation of new ways of organising the work of Commissioners.

2.2 The objectives of centralisation

At the beginning of the process of centralisation the Commission identified its main objectives as follows:

a. To enable the Commission within its budget to carry out its statutory functions (see Chapter 1) and the monitoring of the Code of Practice (see Chapter 8) in as effective and efficient a manner as possible and also with as great a national consistency as is possible.

b. To enable the Commission to make a more effective contribution at a general policy level on issues relevant to its statutory remit by, in part, making more use of the information acquired by members of the Commission carrying out its statutory functions.

The major task of the Commission in the two years covered by this report has been to continue to carry out its statutory functions with as little disruption as possible, while at the same time implementing the reorganisation.

2.3 Reorganisation and members of the Commission: the new structure

Centralisation meant that the organisation of the work of members of the Commission had to be completely restructured.

At a full Commission meeting on the 30th January 1990, in London, the Commission accepted the following new arrangements:

(a) Commission Visiting Teams (CVTs)

Each Commissioner (with the exception of the Chairman and Vice Chairman) is a member of one of seven CVTs. Each CVT is responsible for Commission visiting to all hospitals (other than the Special Hospitals) and mental nursing homes; meetings with social services departments; and the investigation of complaints in a particular geographical area (usually the area of two regional health authorities — see page . . . for further details). Prior to centralisation two different Commission regions divided responsibility for Wales between them. Now, one CVT takes responsibility for the whole of Wales together with one English Regional Health Authority area. Each CVT is assigned a staff support team (see page . . .) in the Nottingham Office, which also organises the Commission's response to requests for doctors appointed under Part IV of the Mental Health Act. Each CVT has a Convenor appointed from among its membership who takes overall responsibility for the work of the team. In addition, one member also becomes complaints convenor taking responsibility for the handling of complaints by the CVT.

(b) Special Hospital Panels (SHPs)

With the exception of the Chairman and Vice Chairman, each Commissioner is a member of one of three SHPs, each of which relates to one of the three Special Hospitals, (Broadmoor, Ashworth and Rampton). Approximately one third of patients detained under the Mental Health Act are in the Special Hospitals and the Commission has decided to continue its policy of visiting detained patients in those hospitals much more frequently than other hospitals. This is reflected in the creation of separate panels for the undertaking of the Commission's special hospital responsibilities. As with the CVTs, the SHPs have their own convenor and complaints convenor. They also have their own administrative teams who organise the Commission's response to requests from the Special Hospitals for doctors appointed under Part IV of the Mental Health Act.

(c) National Standing Committees (NSCs)

The Commission has established ten National Standing Committees (NSCs). Most Commissioners are members of at least one committee. Three NSCs (Visiting, Consent to Treatment and Complaints) take responsibility for overseeing the three fundamental operational responsibilities of the Commission, as indicated by their respective titles. The other NSCs take responsibility for discrete policy areas and include Race and Culture, Code of Practice and Mentally Disturbed Offenders. A list of NSCs with their respective terms of reference can be found at Appendix 2. The establishment of the NSCs has resulted in the Commission beginning to address more effectively and efficiently the broader policy issues that fall within its remit; an account of some of their activities can be found later in this report.

(d) Central Policy Committee (CPC)

Membership of CPC, which is governed by the provisions of a Statutory Instrument, comprises the Commission Chairman and Vice Chairman and ten other members of the Commission (all appointed by the Secretary of State for Health). It has overall responsibility for the activities of the Commission and in particular for overseeing financial control of the organisation. CPC has a number of specifically designated functions (see Mental Health Act Commission Regulations 1983 — Appendix 1) including responsibility for production of the Biennial Report. The Committee meets approximately once in two months.

2.4 Making centralisation work

An organisation composed of approximately 90 part-time members and with diverse statutory responsibilities is by definition faced with an immense administrative task of co-ordination, not only in carrying out its basic statutory tasks of visiting, dealing with complaints, and with the administration of Part IV of the Mental Health Act, but also in making the best use of its members' knowledge and experience in carrying out these tasks at a broader policy level, particularly in influencing Government, providers of mental health services and mental health professionals. The establishment of the NSCs is intended to improve the Commission's capacity to do this. At a more practical level, two developments during the period under review will contribute to a great focusing of the Commission's administration and its public voice.

(a) Computerisation

In 1990, following the decision to centralise the Commission's administration, it was decided to computerise the Commission's administrative procedures. This work has been undertaken and funded by the Information Services Directorate of the Department of Health. A Project Board (whose membership included the Commission's Chief Executive) was established at the beginning of 1991. At the same time a project manager was appointed and the Commission was provided with funding to appoint one of its Executive Officers as Commission Computer Officer. It had been hoped that the project would be completed by the end of 1991. Financial constraints and the complexity of the Commission's various tasks has meant that completion of the computerisation of the administrative procedures required for the Commission's visiting responsibilities will not be completed until March 1992; the remainder of the task will be completed by March 1993. The process of computerisation has required, and will continue to require, a considerable input from both staff and Commissioners; it has been a major management challenge for the Commission's administration to ensure that this does not interfere with the ongoing work of the Commission. At the same time the process has prompted the Commission to review in great detail its procedures prior to its computerisation.

(b) Provision of advice

From its inception the Commission has received numerous requests for advice and guidance on issues relating to the Mental Health Act. Frequently such requests, which in the main come from mental health professionals and administrators, involve complex issues of both law and practice. Centralisation has made it easier to organise a coherent and consistent response to such requests, and it is appropriate in this report to outline the limits of the Commission's ability to help. While the Commission is always anxious to be of assistance, it is important to recognise that the Commission cannot give formal legal advice. Responsibility for interpreting the law correctly must remain with those exercising powers under the Act and their legal advisors. The Commission can, however, express a view, although it is important to recognise that it is no more than that. Not infrequently, the Commission as a body has not considered an issue raised by a particular query and in those circumstances Commission staff or a Commissioner may be able to offer a personal view which does not in itself constitute a formal Commission position.

One of the great problems encountered by the Commission in responding to the enormous range of queries that it receives has been to ensure that its responses are consistent. Two developments in the period under review will contribute to the achievement of this objective. The Mental Health Act Code of Practice published in 1990 by the Secretary of State for Health and the Secretary of State for Wales provides guidance on many of the issues that are raised with the Commission. At the same time the Department of Health has now agreed that the Commission can, from time to time, publish practice notes. It is envisaged these will set out the Commission's advice on issues about which it receives numerous requests and which are not dealt with in the Code of Practice. It is anticipated that the first will deal with the important issue of the transfer of patients from one hospital to another while they are detained under Section 5 (2) of the Act. It is hoped that such practice notes (which will be made available to those involved in the provision of mental health services as well as to Commissioners and Commission staff) will contribute to the provision of patient care and the due regard for patient rights. Towards the end of the period under review the Department of Health provided the Commission with resources to recruit a Legal Officer. The holder of this post will, among other tasks, be providing the Commission with advice on legal issues arising out of its performance of its statutory remit, and will have particular responsibilities in relation to the production of Commission practice notes.

2.5 Finance

The Mental Health Act Commission, as a Special Health Authority, is financed directly by the Department of Health, with a contribution from the Welsh Office. The Commission's expenditure, which is cash limited in the same way as other health authorities, is summarised at Appendix 3.

The work of the Commission in administering and monitoring the consent to treatment provisions contained in Part IV of the Mental Health Act is required by the Act and this item of expenditure cannot be directly controlled by the Commission. An unexpectedly large number of requests for Second Opinion Appointed Doctors can distort the Commission's overall budget and office workload. It is also important to note that the Commission has no direct control over the number of complaints it receives. Although it can decline to pursue a particular complaint, it continues to be the Commission view that it would be unacceptable to do so for financial reasons.

Responsibility for financial control of the Commission rests with the Central Policy Committee. The Commission's Chief Executive is the Commission's designated finance officer.

2.6 The Commission in Wales

Mae y Comisiwn wedi penderfynu cael papur ysgrifennu newydd i'w ddefnyddio pan yn cysylltu yn ysgrifenedig gydag asiantau ac ysbytai yng Nghymru. Mae enw y Comisiwn yn cael ei gynnig yn ddwy-ieithog ar ben y llythyr.

Hefyd mae y Comisiwn yn ddiolchgar i'r Swyddfa Gymreig am benodi, yn ddiweddar, ddau berson i weithio ar y Comisiwn, a'r rheiny yn Gymry Cymraeg. Fe fyddant yn gweithio yn arbennig mewn ysbytai ac Asiantau Gwaith Cymdeithasol yng Nghymru.

The Commission has decided to obtain new headed notepaper for use in written communications with organisations in Wales. The Commission also welcomes the recent appointment of two Commissioners who are Welsh speakers. The new Commissioners will, in particular, be visiting hospitals and mental nursing homes in Wales as well as meeting with Welsh Social Services Departments.

2.7 The Challenge for Staff

The transfer of the Commission's administration to a single office in Nottingham during 1990 presented the Commission's administration with a major challenge. With one exception no members of staff transferred from the closed London and Liverpool offices and only two of the regional office staff in Nottingham had any length of service with the Commission. The key to the successful induction of staff with no previous experience of work in the mental health field has been training; during the latter part of the period covered by this report an extensive training program has been undertaken, conducted by Commissioners, senior Commission staff and external training agencies.

DISTRIBUTION OF COMMISSION VISITING TEAMS

CVT   Regional Health Authority Area/Wales

1. East Anglia/NE Thames
2. North West Thames/Oxford
3. South East Thames/South West Thames
4. Wessex/South Western
5. Trent/Yorkshire and Northern
6. Wales/West Midlands
7. Mersey/North Western

MHAC
ADMINISTRATION

Maid Marian House
56 Hounds Gate
Nottingham
NG1 6BG

Tel: 0602 504040
Fax: 0602 505998

3.
VISITS TO HOSPITALS (OTHER THAN SPECIAL HOSPITALS) AND MENTAL NURSING HOMES AND MEETINGS WITH SOCIAL SERVICES DEPARTMENTS

3.1 Visits to Hospitals and Mental Nursing Homes

The Commission visits patients detained under the Mental Health Act in hospitals, Special Hospitals (see Chapter 4), mental nursing homes, and units spanning the whole range of provisions for in-patient care. The three previous Biennial Reports have described in considerable detail the purpose of visits and how they have been organised. In the two years under review the following visits were undertaken.

	Hospitals	Mental Nursing Homes
Announced visits	961	52
Announced visits "out of hours"	5	–
Unannounced visits	4	1
Total visits	970	53
Total units in programme	557	57

On average each hospital or mental nursing home is visited by members of the Commission once a year. Units that provide care for patients detained under the Mental Health Act in conditions of high security (for example Regional Secure Units and some secure mental nursing homes in the private sector) are visited more frequently. In such establishments patient freedoms are self evidently subject to greater curtailment and the more frequent visits provide members of the Commission with opportunity to keep under review the progress of those patients who during their detention require various degrees of security in different hospitals or units.

The Commission has continued to meet with District and Regional Health Authorities and also the Welsh Office to consider issues unresolved at hospital level or which have wider implications better examined at a higher level.

A number of the issues that arise from such visits are referred to later in this chapter.

3.2 Meetings with Social Services Departments

The Commissioners have continued to meet with Social Services Department at least once every two years to discuss the operation of statutory assessment and admission procedures for people requiring detention under the Mental Health Act and the effectiveness of their compliance with the after-care provisions of Section 117 of the Act. Members of the Commission continue to pay particular attention to the use made of guardianship. Some issues arising from such meetings are referred to in Chapter 13.

3.3 Joint Visits to Hospitals and Meetings with Social Services Departments

The trend, reported in the Third Biennial Report, of joint visits by Commissioners to services provided by health authorities and social services departments with coterminous boundaries have continued with the obvious advantage of being able to comment on the full service offered to detained patients.

3.4 How the Commission Visits

The Commission's Visiting NSC has undertaken the task of standardising visiting policy and procedures. The procedures cover hospitals, mental nursing homes, special hospitals and meetings with Social Services Department and include procedures to be adopted on joint visits. Implementation of the new procedures should result in the systematic and coherent planning and organisation of visits and meetings resulting in a more efficient standardisation of information sought by the Commission and of issues that will be the subject of attention on future visits. The impending computerisation of the Commission's visiting procedures will make a major contribution to the achievement of those objectives and hopefully the more systematic collation of information gathered on visits will enable the Commission to speak with greater authority about the issues that arise during the undertaking of this particular Commission statutory responsibility.

Centralisation and the consequent review of the visiting procedures has raised questions about the adequacy with which the Commission fulfills its statutory function of visiting detained patients. If Commissioners visit most hospitals and mental nursing homes once a year but patients remain detained for an average no more than 21 days, it will be apparent that most patients never have the opportunity to see a Commissioner. It is the Commission's view that this is an unsatisfactory state of affairs which will be drawn to the attention of Ministers.

The rapid changes in the way mental health care is delivered and in particular the closure of large psychiatric hospitals with their replacement by smaller units, is producing a rapid increase in the number of hospitals and mental nursing homes capable of receiving detained patients. For example, in spite of closures of large hospitals, the number of NHS hospitals in the Commission visiting program has actually increased from 437 in the period 1987 to 1989 to 557 in the current biennial period. This development will present the Commission with a considerable challenge to the efficiency with which it undertakes its visiting responsibility.

3.5 Outcome of Visits

The standardisation of Commission Visiting Procedures should result in greater attention being paid to measuring the impact of its visits and a higher degree of focus on issues to be reviewed by Commissioners on their visits. For example all Commission visits after June 1990 paid particular attention to the availability of the Code of Practice and training for mental health staff in its use. It is proposed that in future all Commission visits will examine one or two identified issues as well as others specific to a particular visit. This should enable the Commission to address with greater authority particular problems, relevant to its remit and about which it is concerned.

3.6 Issues Affecting Patients in Hospitals and Mental Nursing Homes

In its approximately four hundred visits to hospitals per year the Commission encountered a wide range of issues, many of which can be found elsewhere in this report. Set out below are a number of matters that arise immediately out of visits to hospitals.

(a) Physical standards of wards

Members of the Commission continue to encounter unacceptable standards, especially in hospitals in the course of closure. A visit to Rainhill Hospital revealed one ward for 31 mentally ill long stay patients in a dismal state of deterioration, with what appeared to be damp walls, broken chairs and only two baths positioned at the entrance to the ward, with a torn curtain and a broken curtain rail which deprived patients of any privacy. Another ward on the second floor, approached by a cement spiral staircase which appeared to have been used on occasions as a lavatory, was in equally bad condition. Strong representation from the Commission and voluntary agencies led to the wards being closed within a week and at a follow-up visit one month later Commissioners were pleased to note that many of the patients had been transferred to new community facilities and that those remaining were in greatly improved surroundings. Commissioners were similarly concerned about the physical environment for detained patients at Littlemoor Hospital in Oxford in February 1991 and advised the Health Authority that three units within the hospital were unfit to receive detained patients. Immediate improvements were implemented by the Health Authority in advance of the start of a major new building scheme which had been delayed by a collapse in the value of health authority land, whose sale was to fund the scheme. The Commission is fully aware of the resource difficulties faced by health authorities, in the process of moving towards a community based service. The Commission's concern is restricted to the impact of such difficulties on detained patients and any resolution must lie in other hands. It is, however, a matter of grave concern that the Commission is at times forced to conclude that some units and wards are unfit for detained patients. Case 1 sets out activities in Hackney and illustrates similar problems.

(b) The use of Section 5 (2)

In the third Biennial Report (page 54) the Commission anticipated that it would be unnecessary in this report to express concerns about the continued misuse of Section 5 (2). The clear guidance in the Code of Practice has undoubtedly contributed to an improvement in practice by Health Authorities and professionals. Concern still remains however, especially in relation to its use at times when insufficient professionals are available to enable an assessment for admission under Section 2 to be undertaken. Recent research in a mid-Glamorgan hospital (correspondence Psychiatric Bulletin (April 1991 pp. 224-225)) revealed that Friday was the most common day for its use. There are still occasions when the patient remains on the detention order for the full period without assessment or remains on the order after assessment has been completed.

The Commission will continue to pay attention to the use of Section 5 (2).

(c) Deaths of detained patients

The Commission continues to depute one of its members to attend most inquests on the death of a detained patient. In the past the Commission has asked all hospitals to inform it of such deaths in advance of any inquest and a reminder will shortly be sent out to all health authorities, relevant NHS Trusts and Mental Nursing Homes. Commissioners attend inquests as observers and with a view to identifying any information in the evidence that is relevant to the Commission's statutory responsibilities. In the next two years the Commission proposes, with the assistance of the improved information collating system that will result from centralisation, to identify more effectively the common issues surrounding such deaths.

(d) Child and Adolescent Psychiatric Units

In the period under review the Commission has visited a number of NHS and private units providing psychiatric care for children and young people. The Commission visits such units because they are capable of receiving detained patients, although it appears to be rare that patients are detained under the Act. Frequently patients are the subject of child care orders or are placed there by their parents. One particular unit was Langton House in Dorset, a mental nursing home run by a private company. In all, six different official agencies had an interest in how the unit operated and a high level of collaboration between them was achieved in presenting their joint concerns in a co-ordinated manner to the proprietors who implemented much of what was asked of them. In June the proprietors decided to close the unit as they felt unable to operate the new regime satisfactorily.

The lack of legal clarity about the circumstances in which competent children can be treated against their wishes when they are detained other than under the Mental Health Act was identified as an important issue, as well as the implementation of appropriate safeguards. The Children Act will make a contribution to improving the situation, but the Commission will be considering this matter in greater detail in the future.

(e) Racial issues
(i) Patients

The Commission, through its visiting teams, continues to ask hospitals to provide ethnic data on detained patients but many still fail to do so. Further, it is very disappointing to note that, in spite of the advice given in the Second and Third Biennial Reports of the Commission, it is still relatively rare to see a mental health service in which there is a senior member of staff designated to take responsibility for ensuring that the different needs of black and ethnic minorities are taken into account in service provision. One leading example of a district that is establishing structures that may lead to better services for ethnic minorities is Parkside Health Authority in London. This purchasing authority has made it a requirement that all providers of mental health services have a system of ethnic monitoring and the current provider of these services has an adviser who liaises with a counterpart on the purchasing side.

The Commission recommends that purchasing authorities require providers to monitor the ethnicity of detained patients and ensure that mental health services develop clear guidelines on promoting culturally sensitive services.

The relatively high level of compulsory admission of Afro-Caribbean people noted in the Second and Third Biennial Reports of the Commission, appears to be continuing. (Noble and Rodger, 1989; Bowl and Barnes, 1990). There may also be a disproportionate number of Afro-Caribbean patients in RSUs and the locked wards of psychiatric hospitals. Community groups have expressed concern that Afro-Caribbean patients may be given higher doses of medication than other patients. This is partly born out by a study in Nottingham by Chen, Harrison and Standen (1991) which reported that a subgroup of Afro-Caribbean patients received higher peak doses of depot medication than other patients. Health Authorities are urged to review the priority they afford to mental health services for the Afro-Caribbean population.

Bowl, R and Barnes M (1990) Approved Social Work Assessments, Race and Racism: Local Authority Policy and Practice. Social Services Research Group.

Chen, E Y H, Harrison, G and Standen P J (1991) Management of First Episode Psychotic Illness in Afro-Caribbean patients. British Journal of Psychiatry, 158, 517-22.

Noble P and Rodger S E (1989) Violence by Psychiatric In-patients. British Journal of Psychiatry, 155, 384-90.

(ii) Information about Rights
The extent to which detained patients are informed about their rights depends on the ease of communication between patients and staff and this is a particular problem in the case of patients whose first language is not English. Since the provision of rights leaflets in various languages may help in easing this problem the Commission is pleased that Chinese, Hindi, Polish, Punjabi and Vietnamese versions of patient leaflets prepared by the Department of Health are now available (from The Health Publication Branch, Room 202A, Eileen House, 80-94 Newington Causeway, London) and that Bengali, Gujerati and Urdu versions have also been prepared and will be available shortly. The Commission will monitor the usefulness of these leaflets as well as consider the desirability of encouraging the provision of the leaflets in other languages.

(iii) Staffing of Mental Health Services
The credibility of a service to a multi-ethnic population depends on the extent to which its staffing structure represents the ethnic diversity of the catchment population. Although many health districts have equal opportunities policies for employment applicable to most staff appointments, there are relatively few people from black and ethnic minorities in managerial positions in the mental health services. Also, there appears to be a paucity of senior medical staff from black and ethnic minority communities in the Health Districts that deal with the inner city boroughs in London where many of these communities are concentrated. The Commission recommends that Health Authorities address these staffing issues as a matter of some urgency.

At the grass roots level of service provision, many professionals seem to lack basic knowledge about the different needs of ethnic minority communities and have little real understanding of institutional racism and the effects of cultural differences on the nature of mental disorder. This applies even in areas where there are relatively large numbers of people from one or more ethnic minorities. Clearly, deficiencies in professioal training need to be addressed and we recommend that the Royal Colleges and other professional bodies should ensure the training in this area is improved.

Further issues relating to Mental Nursing Homes are contained in Chapter 13.

The Community

Community care in Hackney is both well advanced and well developed. Since the inception of the Community Psychiatry Research Unit (CPRU) in 1979 an expanding number of projects have concentrated on three areas of work; first, development of a wide range of housing options; second, long term support in the community to individuals with serious mental disorder; and thirdly, the coordination and monitoring of local services by developing computerised information systems based on a register of all those in contact with the service.

The achievements of the Unit are outstanding. There is now a range of flats, hostels and staffed homes that, by the end of 1991, will be providing 24 hour care for ninety or so very dependent people. There are a further 37 single flats and five family flats where residents are supported by CPRU.

Hackney is a long way off meeting their own accommodation targets but they have gone further to meet the need locally than any other inner city service.

The Hackney Hospital was built as a workhouse in 1860. All its services, except psychiatry and elderly (7 wards) were transferred four years ago to the Homerton District General Hospital. The proposed date for phase 2 of the Homerton development was 1994/95. This no longer applies and no new date has been agreed.

The Hospital

The unit comprises the following beds
— 50 Acute
— 70 Elderly Mentally Ill
— 20 Rehabilitation
— 8 Intensive Care
— 12 Secure Units

There are a further 20 acute beds located on Strauss Ward at St Bartholomew's. In the period 1989-91 the catchment population was 193,000. The annual total of pateints on section was:

1984 (January-December) = 228
1987 (January-December) = 280
1990/1 (January-March)   = 465

More than 50% of these patients were from ethnic minorities. On any one day in 1990/91 the number on section in all but the wards for the elderly mentally ill was approximately 48. This represents 47% of the total. The figures in 1990/91 for patients on Court Orders was 50:

Sections 35/36/38 = 12
Sections 37/47/48 = 20

Sections 37/41   = 18
Sections 136/47/49 = 96

The 18 patients on Sections 37/41 are dependent upon Home Office decisions for their transfer and such a large number put great pressure on existing beds.

The 12-bedded Interim Secure Unit serves five London districts. The City and Hackney Health Authority accounts for 51% of all admissions. A total of 23 patients are placed in out-of-district private facilities — 9 patients who are assessed and not meeting secure unit criteria are funded by the district and 14 by the Region. The cost per annum represents 20% of the total budget for mental health services in Hackney.

Commission concerns

1. When health services were reprovided in 1986 at Homerton Hospital, psychiatric services remained in the original buildings.
2. Those services are only able to cater for the most disturbed patients.
3. There are no long stay facilities.
4. The forensic services are inadequate to meet demand.
5. There appears to be a significant increase in the use of detention.

Finances

National figures indicate that an average 16% of Health Authority budgets are expended on mental health services. In Hackney:

a. The mental health budget for acute and elderly patient services is £8.8m. The total budget allocated for Hackney residents is £71m and the mental health element constitutes 12% of the budget or three-quarters of the National average.

b. The Regional Health Authority has not yet decided the allocation of funds to the five districts for the purchase of places in the Secure Unit.

The Commission

In 1985 a Commission report stated:

"Commissioners acknowledged the seriousness of the Health Authorities difficulty in providing an adequate service within present resources". Subsequently the Commission have visited the Secure Unit every six months and the Hackney Unit every nine months. Its reports to the District General Manager have reflected the growing seriousness of the problems. The Commission is cognisant of the seriousness with which the Regional Health Authority views the problems of Hackney and the efforts it is now making to overcome them.

Each year since 1987 the Commission has met with the Regional Health Authority and drawn attention to the very poor conditions in which patients are detained.

Latterly the Commission has attended a local public meeting arranged by the Community Health Council and Hackney MIND and written direct to the Secretary of State. In this letter the Commissioners stated "The wards providing acute care were very hot, smelly and sleeping accommodation extremely cramped. In one ward the bed provided was not long enough for the patient who occupied it. Additionally, a mother and baby unit is housed on the fourth floor of this block and patients are denied exercise and fresh air for themselves and their offspring.

On both the acute and elderly wards the provision of toilet and bathing facilities are minimal. On one ward (Hanover) at night there are two toilets for 18 patients, many of whom suffer from problems with micturition. Beds are often separated from each other only by flimsy curtains and privacy especially on mixed wards is impossible to sustain.

The effect of the conditions on patient and staff morale is considerable; the drab surroundings and environment are neither therapeutic nor appropriate for some of the most disturbed mentally ill patients in the Hackney Health Authority".

Gaps in provision

— Forensic services are underprovided;
— Rehabilitation services are seriously depleted;
— The Hackney Hospital has received no money for general maintenance. The wards are in very poor decorative state. The heating system is obsolete.
— The ward environments are continuously disturbed because of
— a lack of facilities
— no access to exercise
— the high numbers of very disturbed patients
— cramped conditions
— poor patient mix

The following receive no services either in the unit or the district:
— Difficult-to-place patients
— Patients with brain damage

The future for Hackney

The present suggestion of reproviding mental health services up to a maximum of £10m by superimposing them on existing sites at the Homerton and St Bartholomew's is a short term measure.

The revenue budget for mental health services requires immediate revision to bring it in line with the National average and to provide special funds for deprived catchment area.

The Commission is concerned that capital funding is so dependent upon the vagaries of land values. The attention of Parliament is drawn to the need for capital funding of £60m to complete phase 2 to provide adequate facilities for the high numbers of patients being detained under the Mental Health Act.

Case 1

4.
VISITING THE SPECIAL HOSPITALS

4.1 Introduction

The three Special Hospitals, Broadmoor, Rampton and Ashworth (formerly Park Lane and Moss Side which were amalgamated on 1st July 1989) provide care and treatment for approximately one third of all patients detained under the Mental Health Act. While most patients in Special Hospitals are detained under Part III of the Act (resulting from criminal proceedings) one third of patients enter by way of civil admission under Part II of the Act where there have been no criminal proceedings. The most significant event in the period under review has been the establishment of the Special Hospitals Service Authority (SHSA) on the 1st July 1989. This is a Special Health Authority and has taken overall responsibility for the management of the Special Hospitals from the previous local hospital boards (see third Biennial Report). The Commission warmly welcomes the creation of the authority.

4.2 Visits to the Special Hospitals

In the period under review the Commission made the following visits to the Special Hospitals:

Announced visits	183
Unannounced visits	—
Total visits	183
Total hospitals in programme	3

(a) Broadmoor Hospital

Visiting arrangements have remained generally the same as reported in the Second Biennial Report. The Broadmoor Special Hospital Panel (SHP) has been sub-divided into teams of 6-7 Commissioners who visit allocated houses approximately every eight to ten weeks. Each team takes responsibility for liaising with a particular department with the hospitals. The SHP Convenor, the Complaints Convenor and the team leaders periodically meet with the Hospital Management Team to follow up issues arising from visits to wards and houses.

(b) Rampton Hospital

The Rampton SHP is divided into a number of small teams which visit allocated clinical units within the hospital. Like Broadmoor the SHP Convenor, the Complaints Convenor and the team leaders periodically meet with the Hospital Management Team.

(c) Ashworth Hospital

The reorganisation of the Commission coincided with the amalgamation of Park Lane and Moss Side into a single hospital — Ashworth Hospital. Previously, members of the Commission allocated to the North West region each belonged to the two visiting teams, one for Park Lane Hospital (now Ashworth North) and the other for Moss Side (now Ashworth South). The Commission's new visiting arrangements involve a multidisciplinary panel of Commissioners representing approximately one third of all Commissioners, who are divided into five teams to relate to the Senior Clinical Nurse Managers within Ashworth, each team visiting wards in both Ashworth North and Ashworth South. The large numbers of wards on a campus with three separate security systems and two Medical Records offices,

still functioning largely independently, has created some problems.

A programme of periodic meetings with the Hospital Management Team considering an agreed agenda has now been established, supported by meetings between the Commission visiting teams and the clinical teams for the units within Ashworth Hospital. The many departments providing rehabilitation and services are also allocated to the visiting teams and the new structure has provided an opportunity for Commissioners to visit these areas systematically.

4.3 The Commission and the Special Hospitals Service Authority (SHSA)

The establishment of the SHSA has prompted the Commission to review its relationship to the Special Hospitals generally and has provided an improved framework within which the Commission can pursue its statutory remit. The Commission's primary statutory responsibility in relation to the Special Hospitals is to visit patients detained in the hospitals. The bulk of Commission activity therefore, takes place at ward or unit level by way of Commission visits. Many of the issues raised on such visits are dealt with at that level. Not infrequently unresolved concerns or those which raise broader policy issues are taken up at the periodic meetings with the hospital management teams. Into this framework has been introduced biennial meetings with the SHSA, at which discussions about selected topics of especial concern to the Commission can be raised. For example the Commission's profound anxieties about the continued existence of "slopping out" (see page 21) have been raised. The reorganisation of the management of the Special Hospitals has led to the establishment at each hospital of a Hospital Advisory Committee (HAC). These committees, composed of people independent of the hospital, undertake the functions of the statutory Mental Health Act Managers (for example to consider requests for review of detention by patients detained under Part II of the Act) and have an important role in relation to monitoring the operation of the complaint's procedures within the hospitals. The committees have been establishing themselves throughout the period under review and in June 1991 the Chief Executive spoke at the first conference organised by the SHSA for HAC members. The Commission is currently exploring with each HAC how the Commission can best liaise with them in pursuit of the Commission's statutory responsibilities. One of the first tasks of the Commission after centralisation was to establish a single visiting policy for the Special Hospitals; during the period under review such a policy was agreed with the SHSA (see Appendix 4).

The Commission has in the past been criticised for becoming involved in what many might regard as trivial complaints at ward level at the expense of broader and substantive issues that relate to the whole Special Hospital system. What may seem trivial may in fact be of profound importance to a patient detained for long periods in a high security institution, such as a Special Hospital, and it is therefore right that the Commission continues to pursue such matters. There is, however, some truth in the criticism made and it is hoped that the new coherence of the management structures of both the Special Hospitals and Commission will contribute to an increase in the effectiveness of the Commission's performance of its statutory responsibilities.

4.4 The Special Hospitals — general issues

(a) The Code of Practice

One of the first major topics discussed with the SHSA was compliance by the Special Hospitals with the Code of Practice. The Commission was and remains concerned about two specific issues:

i. The use of seclusion; and

ii. the undertaking by the HACs of responsibilities arising from their duties as Mental Health Act Managers (a task allocated to the HACs [see above]).

Since its establishment the Commission has been gravely concerned about the way in which seclusion is used in the Special Hospitals. There has never been a common definition of seclusion throughout the Special Hospital System nor a common seclusion policy. Anxiety about the use of seclusion is shared by the SHSA and the Commission welcomed their proposal to undertake a major research initiative. This will clearly take some time but, the view of the Commission is that immediate action is required. The Mental Health Act Code of Practice contains extensive guidance about the use of seclusion and the Commission takes the fairly straightforward approach that it is as applicable to the Special Hospitals as to other hospitals. The SHSA has reported to the Commission difficulties (relating to the frequency of use, the number of detained patients and inadequate staffing levels) in complying with the safeguards in the Code, although the Commission understands that full compliance is their ultimate target. Whilst the Commission recognises such difficulties there is no reason why the Secretary of State's guidance contained in the Code should not apply in full to the Special Hospitals and the Commission will continue to press for its early implementation.

The Act gives to the Mental Health Act Managers important statutory responsibilities, including the exercise of an independent power to discharge patients detained under Part II (civilly detained patients). The Code of Practice contains extensive guidance on the undertaking of such responsibilities and it has become clear to the Commission that the HACs are not yet adequately resourced to comply with the Code fully in this respect. The Commission is impressed with the efforts being made by the HACs to follow the Code (they are a considerable improvement on the situation before their establishment) and will be pressing for full compliance so that patients therein receive the same consideration as patients detained in most hospitals.

(b) Slopping out

In the Third Biennial Report concern was expressed about the necessity for many patients in the Special Hospitals to "slop out", due to lack of access to lavatories during the night. Towards the end of the period under review this matter was highlighted by the Home Secretary's undertaking to end the practice in prisons by 1994 and the Commission took the opportunity to express publicly its concern about this practice in the Special Hospitals. The Commission welcomes the recognition by the SHSA that this is an unacceptable facet of Special Hospital life and has noted that within three years it is intended that 40% of patients will have private sanitation. This will be achieved in the main by capital expenditure. The practice will not, however, be eliminated by capital expenditure alone, although acceptable private sanitation facilities for the majority of patients would be desirable. "Slopping out" is also a consequence of night staffing levels, insufficient to enable patients to be escorted to a lavatory when necessary. The Commission regards "slopping out" as wholly unacceptable in any hospital and will continue to press the SHSA to bring it to an end as a matter of urgency. The Commission strongly urges the SHSA and the Department of Health to immediately set target dates for the phasing out of "slopping out" and the provision of acceptable alternatives no later than those set for the prisons.

(c) Transfer delays

All three previous Biennial Reports expressed grave concern at the difficulties experienced in transfer of patients from Special Hospitals to other units (e,g. Regional Secure Units [RSU] or ordinary hospitals) or (more rarely) the community. Despite some progress this remains an area of continuing concern which the SHSA shares with the Commission. The establishment by the Authorities of a monthly return of patients on the transfer list, setting out progress against time limits, is welcomed, as is the proposed publication of a guide to the transfer process for patients. The reasons for delay remain the same as in the past; a review of the Commission's recent experience at Broadmoor Hospital reveal the following contributory factors:

i. A change in a patient's Responsible Medical Officer (RMO) may result in a considerable delay while he or she considers whether to endorse previous recommendations; frequent changes of RMO can result in substantial delays;

ii. The Home Secretary will now only consider authorising the transfer of a restricted patient if the SHSA has indicated its approval; the addition of this extra component to the process has led to increased delay;

iii. The apparent shortage of beds in RSUs and other secure units is a significant cause of delays in transferring Special Hospital patients. The reality is that such patients compete with those requiring admission from courts, prisons and ordinary hospitals, whose priority is often regarded as greater.

Transfer delays are detrimental not only to the interests of the patients concerned, but also those caring for them. To jeopardize patient treatment in this way is unacceptable. The Commission continues to press for solutions to this problem in a number of ways, including:

i. responding to the consultation document shortly to be published by the Home Office/Department of Health Committees reviewing services for mentally disordered offenders:

ii. continuing to follow-through individual cases of transfer delay on visits to hospitals and secure units;

iii. establishing a working group in the summer of 1991 to analyse in depth transfer delays in Ashworth Hospital in the same way as the Commission did for Rampton (Second Biennial Report, page 37) and Moss Side (Third Biennial Report page 30). Both these studies made a major contribution to the identification of the reasons for delay.

In the Third Biennial Report the Commission was highly critical of the lack of secure facilities in Wales and the impact of this on special hospital patients from Wales awaiting transfer. Whilst the absence of an all Wales Forensic Service is a matter of concern, the Commission welcomes the development of an interim regional secure unit at Glan Rhyd Hospital, Bridgend, by the end of 1991 and the forthcoming publication of the Forensic Services Working Party report, commissioned by the Welsh Office.

Elsewhere in this report (see Chapter 10) there is a brief discussion of transfer delays affecting special hospital patients with learning disabilities or mental handicap.

(d) Women in the Special Hospitals

The admission to, and provision of care of, women in the Special Hospitals has caused the Commission concern in the period under review; a concern shared by the SHSA, (which has set up a working party to consider the provision of services to women patients in Broadmoor while a multi-disciplinary working party is examining the issues at Ashworth) and voluntary groups. One of the Ashworth Special Hospital Panel visiting teams concentrate on visiting female wards and has paid special attention to the position of women patients.

A worryingly high proportion of women admitted to the Special Hospitals in recent years has been aged 20 or under. The Commission is concerned that more appropriate placements should be available for some of the younger women now in the Special Hospitals. Nevertheless the Commission recognises that there are women for whom no satisfactory alternative placement currently exists, but stresses that services within the Special Hospitals should be developed appropriately to meet their special needs. There are a number of specific issues relating to women patients which the Commission wishes to raise.

(i) Self harm

The incidence of self harm amongst the women patients at Ashworth is disturbingly high. The Commission has similar concerns about Broadmoor. Many women patients suffer from a serious lack of self-esteem and feelings of powerlessness. Such feelings can be reinforced by the way in which women's lives are controlled within the institution.

The Commission welcomes the fact that the psychology department at Ashworth Hospital is trying to develop both understanding and action on this issue, and that a multi-disciplinary group within the hospital is looking at issues relating to women patients. Management action is needed to ensure that all disciplines are working with common understandings, values and purpose in order to provide a consistent regime which will enhance self esteem and enable women to develop appropriate control over their lives.

(ii) Male nursing of women patients

In recent years there has been a welcome move to mix the gender of staff on both male and female wards in special Hospitals. However, the introduction of male staff on female wards has not always been carried out sensitively. Male staff have not been adequately trained and the staffing mix is sometimes inappropriate. There should always be sufficient women staff to manage the personal 'hands-on' care needs of women patients. The Commission also would like to see more women charge nurses who can demonstrate a positive image of women in positions of responsibility. Sufficient women staff will also enable women patients who, find it difficult or unhelpful to discuss their concerns with men to identify a member of the ward staff to whom they can talk on a day to day basis.

(iii) Mixed rehabilitation wards

Experience of living on a mixed ward is often required of both men and women before patients can be transferred to RSU's or elsewhere. Patients and some staff have expressed fears that women are placed there partly to test out whether male offenders can behave appropriately in a mixed environment. The commission suggest that further thought needs to be given to these perceptions, particularly in view of the high proportion of women in special hospitals who have been sexually abused.

The Commission has previously welcomed the work that has been done to develop integrated wards in the Special Hospitals, but believes that a woman's expressed wishes about transfer to a mixed ward should be given proper weight and the opportunities for women to be transferred out of hospital should not be adversely affected if they would prefer to stay on an all-women's ward.

(iv) Choice of clothes

The availability of a choice of clothes is an issue which continues to be raised with Commissioners by women patients. The particular issue which has come up recently concerns the availability of track suits in a choice of colours and styles. The hospitals keep supplies of track suits designed for men, but not for women. Clothing is an important way of expressing identity and can be a factor influencing feelings of self-esteem. It is important that women are able to choose clothing which they feel is appropriate for themselves.

(v) Language

Language is an important indicator of attitude. Women in Special Hospitals are commonly referred to as 'girls' and some patients have suggested that considerably more abusive language is used on occasions. If the women are to feel that they are being treated with respect by those who have responsibility for their care, the use of non-demeaning language is vital.

It is clear that radical changes are necessary if women in Special Hospitals are to receive the type of care which improves their mental health and also enables them to rebuild their lives when they are discharged. A change in the culture of the Special Hospitals which emphasizes the importance of enhancing self-esteem, and encourages patients to take control of their own lives, would have benefits for both women and men patients.

(e) Consistency of ward regimes

The lack of one person with overall responsibility for the regimes in Special Hospital wards has greatly troubled the Commission in the period under review. The experience of patients that aspects of ward routine, including the use of facilities, might vary with each nursing shift has been a continuing cause of tension in wards. In Rampton this issue has been raised with the Hospital Management Team. At Ashworth one of the lessons that emerged from the hospital inquiry into the death of a patient, Stephen Mallalieu, and which is supported by the Commission, is the need to establish a consistent ward regime that does not vary with each nursing shift. The Commission has warmly welcomed the announcement by the SHSA that it intends to appoint ward managers for each ward in the special hospitals to ensure greater consistency.

(f) Industrial action

For a period of several weeks at the end of 1990 and early in 1991, industrial action was taken by the Prison Officers Association over a dispute with the Special Hospital Service Authority concerning assisted travel payments. The substance of the dispute was not a matter for the Commission but its potential effect on detained patients was of great concern since it involved severe restrictions on patients' activities including outside visits and visits to patients by relatives and professionals. After consultation with the SHSA, the Commission decided to monitor the effect on patients by greatly increasing the intensity of visiting at Rampton and Ashworth where the industrial action took place.

Visiting Commissioners reported some surprising experiences. A "Dunkirk" spirit appeared to prevail amongst the remaining professional and administrative staff. In consequence patients reported that although occupational activities and visits were curtailed they were given greater responsibilities in their wards. Staff talked to them more and the quality and temperature of their food were improved.

Frequently several patients were escorted by only one member of staff without incident and this experience has called into question the traditional manning level which has required at least two staff to escort all patients between departments no matter what their condition. Compliance with this policy often significantly reduces ward activities and the availability of skilled staff and is thus adversely affects patient care. One benefit from the industrial action at Rampton has been a review of escort arrangements aimed at relating the number of escorts to the needs of individual patients.

Commissioners were greatly impressed by the commitment and dedication of these staff who strove to maintain, and in some respects even improve, the quality of patient care during the dispute. They also commend the determined efforts to be overcome the resulting backlog of home visits and shopping trips.

(g) Displays of racist materials

Commissioners have been alarmed at evidence reported to them about the public display of racist propaganda produced by extreme political organisations. Expressions of concern have prompted the removal of such material when it has been seen. Such displays are wholly unacceptable especially in view of the significant number of black patients in the Special Hospitals.

4.5 Individual Special Hospital reports

(a) Broadmoor Special Hospital

The move of some patients to the new Norfolk and Somerset House units (phase 1 of the new development plan) with their single rooms and private sanitary facilities has enabled patient care to become more personalised. The nursing staff are working to achieve a more therapeutic atmosphere on the wards. The building itself has presented various problems: some wards have restricted access to the open air and there are problems with the heating and ventilation system. Ironically, patients in the new houses are facing greater restrictions: for instance, those patients with parole status are not allowed outside the new building and have to be escorted to the parole area in the older parts of the hospital.

The quality of the environment in those areas of the hospital which have not been upgraded, is inadequate for long-term living. Dormitory areas in Dorset and Essex Houses are overcrowded and lacking in privacy to the extent that the quality of patients' lives is seriously affected.

Some individual rooms in Essex House still have no heating. Work is underway to enable heaters to be installed but the age and size of the buildings make this an extremely protracted undertaking.

There is a shortage of interview rooms on many wards. This causes difficulties not only for visiting Commissioners, solicitors, and doctors, but also for hospital staff who do not have the necessary facilities for interviewing patients or carrying out individual treatment programmes.

(i) Policies

The genesis of the new hospital management team has resulted in the production of a number of new policy documents. These are to be welcomed but the Commission is concerned that care should be given to the implementation and monitoring of these policies especially in the case of potentially controversial procedures such as the searching of patients.

An equal opportunities policy is being produced. The Commission hopes that in addition to ensuring equality of opportunity for staff, the fundamental issue of equality of treatment for patients from all ethnic groups will be addressed, recognising that this is a broad issue of concern within mental health services.

(ii) Seclusion

A positive result of the introduction of a new hospital seclusion policy has been the monitoring of seclusion throughout the hospital. This has enabled the positive effects of the move to the new buildings in terms of reduced seclusion to be clearly demonstrated. The monitoring of seclusion has also revealed certain concerns about the treatment of women patients. (see above).

In addition, there has been a small minority of patients who have consistently spent more than 28 days out of each 3 month period in seclusion. The failure of any treatment approach significantly to improve the quality of life of these patients is most regrettable.

Commissioners reviewed the seclusion records on Leeds Ward and note the majority of women who were secluded were placed in "protective clothing". Discussion revealed that staff perceived the clothing in question as "non harmful" rather than protective. Commissioners expressed their concern that the placement of patients in protective clothing appears to be the normal practice on Leeds Ward. On referring to the seclusion policy Commissioners found that the policy states that

"if in the interests of safety, security or hygiene it is necessary to remove patients' clothing, then pyjamas and slippers will be provided".

A working party has been set up to consider the Code of Practice. The Commission hopes that the seclusion policy will be amended to comply with the Code.

(iii) General issues

The Commission is concerned by the lack of flexibility in the patients' daily routine. It was therefore pleased to note that management is now actively encouraging more flexibility within wards at weekends to enable patients to stay in bed longer and, if appropriate, to prepare their own breakfasts.

The Commission has also been dismayed at some of the apparently trivial restrictions imposed on patients, particularly in the admission wards. Consequently it was encouraged when, after some months of negotiation, patients were allowed to wear watches.

The Commission has aslo been pleased to note the introduction of pay phones in some wards.

(iv) Confidentiality

Following two incidents when confidential information concerning patients appeared in the press, the Commission raised the question of leaks by staff. They were reassured to hear that notices had been circulated to all staff emphasizing that any member of staff who divulged information concerning patients to the media would face dismissal. The commission believes the protection of patients' privacy is of utmost importance and hopes that mangement will vigorously enforce its policy.

(b) Rampton Special Hospital

(i) The new facilities

The MHAC welcomed the opening in March 1991 of the refurbished central wards 'A' at Rampton. Approximately 54 patients have single rooms with a built in area containing a lavatory and hand basin. This is a great improvement allowing patients to dress and undress in privacy and the integral sanitation gives the patients and staff a better quality of life. The decor of the block gives a more therapeutic atmosphere and a better environment for staff and patients alike.

(ii) Patients with hearing impairment

In its contacts with patients in Special Hospitals, the Commission has become aware of some of the particular needs of patients with profound communication difficulties resulting from hearing impairment. There are obvious problems to overcome in ensuring that these patients are aware of and can exercise their rights under the Mental Health Act. Their commication difficulties have implication also for their day to day care, especially in respect of retraining and preparation for future rehabilitation and resettlement.

Rampton Hospital is the Special Hospital chosen to provide care for deaf patients, and Commissioners have been reassured that the Hospital has paid special attention to identifying the needs of these patients and addressing the implications of their handicap for the provision of care. Selected staff have been encouraged to learn techniques for communicating with the deaf and have been supported in their practice of such skills. Whilst it is acknowledged that the provision of such staff have cost implications for the Hospital, the Commission would wish to promote the view that suitably trained staff should be available in sufficient numbers to allow patients reasonable exposure to opportunities of communicating in daily life.

(iii) Night staffing

A series of unnatural deaths at Rampton have highlighted problems of night time staffing. At night time there is normally only one member of staff on the ward. It is hospital policy that the door to a patient's room must not be opened except in the presence of two nurses. Inevitably there is therefore a delay while the member of staff summons assistance from other wards in order that he can open the door. This loss of time could be vital if a patient's life is at risk. Another area of concern is that wards have been left unattended while help is offered elsewhere.

The MHAC has expressed its concern that patients who require maximum security and who present a substantially higher risk of suicide than the general population should have such a low level of night time staff on duty on the ward. Rampton has recently initiated a pilot study where some areas have extra staff resources at night. It is hoped this will be extended throughout the hospital. This extra staffing would hopefully enable more patients to have access to toilet facilities at night and would improve night time observation and patient care.

(c) Ashworth Special Hospital

(i) The Mental Health Act

In the Third Biennial Report reference was made to difficulties experienced at Park Lane by medical staff in particular in fully complying with the requirements of Part IV of the Act. The Commission has continued to pursue the matter and is pleased to report improvement, although there remain problems of interpreting the provisions of the Act in relation to the definition of treatment, consent in relation to medication given "as required", the use of Section 62 and observance of Section 61.

(ii) Rehabilitation

Work of an impressively high standard is being undertaken in the extensive off-ward educational, therapeutic and rehabilitative facilities available on the Ashworth campus. The panel had discussed with the Managers the recurring difficulties in exploiting fully the potential within these expensive and well-equipped facilities. Patient activities are often restricted or cancelled (even to the extent that patients in the Education Department were unable to take external examinations) and these difficulties are generally attributed to staffing problems, especially the demands of escort duty when patients require treatment outside the secure perimeter. Eliminating the many impediments to effective and appropriately planning progressive rehabilitation calls for a high priority, if legitimate therapeutic objections are to be met.

The Commission has commended the Managers of Ashworth Hospital in their endeavours to introduce positive outside influences to the social environment within the hospital. Notable in this respect has been the establishment of the Ashworth Arts Council in conjunction with the Tate Gallery, Liverpool, who were prime movers in an innovative, very successful and well attended Arts in Care Conference held in conjuction with the local arts community which provided patients with an opportunity to display a wide range of artistic and creative talent.

(iii) Physical standards of wards

The Commission is very concerned about the physical conditions of two wards: Beeches and Hawthorns and regards both as being nearly unfit for habitation. Beeches is due for upgrading in the Spring of 1992, but as yet there are no plans for Hawthorns. The Commission has similar, if not quite so serious, concerns about the state of Firs Ward.

(iv) Assessment unit

One of the concerns of the Commissioners visiting Ashworth Hospital was the fact that Tennyson Ward, the designated male assessment unit, was failing to meet its objectives. Discussions with patients and staff revealed that: facilities for a comprehensive assessment were not available on the ward; patients spent considerable periods on the ward without constructive action; appropriate placements in other wards could not be made because of a lack of vacancies (caused by transfer delays) and because the patient's responsible medical officer had to bargain with colleagues for a place to be released. Further difficulties were caused to nursing staff because it was possible for each patient to have a different responsible medical officer, who did not always attend the weekly patient care team meetings and had variable communication with nursing staff. These issues were taken up by the Commissioners with Senior Management Staff.

Progress has been made in reviewing the role of the "parent" responsible medical officer arranging "core" team meetings. Proposals by nursing staff have been made for converting space to provide educational and occupational activities areas and for extending the ward. In addition, a working party on admission procedures has been convened to consider both male and female admissions. These developments, together with the work of the transfer delays group, should enable the agreed objectives of the admissions wards to be met.

(v) Seclusion and restraint garments

The Commissioners have been pleased to note improvement in the regime of a number of wards. In particular they would like to commend Arnold Ward where changes have resulted in a reduction in the use of seclusion.

A small number of patients at Ashworth continue to be nursed for substantial periods in restraint garments in spite of the success of repeated endeavours to establish less restrictive measures. The Commission was pleased to be invited to send two observers to the meetings of the Working Party on the use of restraint garments and to learn of the plans to establish a small intensive therapy area where the four patients principally involved can be nursed in an environment more closely attuned to their extremely difficult to manage behaviour.

(vi) Inquiry into deaths at Ashworth
Since the previous report two patients have been unlawfully killed within Ashworth Hospital North. The Commission reviewed the finding of an independent enquiry established by the SHSA into the first death, and subsequently discussed the implications with the SHSA and with the Chairman of the Enquiry Team, Dr J Higgins. The Commission has accepted the conclusions of this equiry that the ward policy on Owen Ward was not adequate and that greater consistency should be established in the ward management between nursing shifts. The Commission looks forward to the appointment of ward managers with this responsibility in all Special Hospitals during 1992. The circumstances involved in the second unlawful killing which took place on a different ward, remain sub judice.

(vii) The Ashworth Special Hospital Inquiry
Following a documentary transmitted on Channel 4 on 4th March, 1991 and the representations made to Government, the Secretary of State on 25th April 1991 appointed four members of the Commission in their individual capacity, to conduct an independent inquiry into (a) complaints of improper care and ill-treatment of patients as Ashworth Special Hospital, and (b) the manner in which complaints had been handled by the hospital management. The setting up of the Inquiry was made after consultation with the Special Hospital Service Authority (SHSA) to whom a copy of the Committee's report would be submitted.

The Parliamentary Under-Secretary of State for Health, Mr Stephen Dorrell MP, had indicated that it is his wish that in the future the Commission should be given a specific power to carry out a preliminary investigation of such allegations of ill-treatment for the purpose of advising the Secretary of State whether, and if so in what form, any inquiry should be undertaken.

At its binannual meetings in York on 26th April, 1991, the Commission in plenary session warmly welcome the setting up of the Inquiry, recognising that the Commission's work as the recipient of patient complaints and watchdog over patient's interests over the years at Ashworth would form part of the Inquiry's remit. At the preliminary hearing on 21 June 1991 the Commission appeared through its Chief Executive and indicated that it would supply the Inquiry with all relevant documentation.

5.
THE INVESTIGATION OF COMPLAINTS

5.1 The Commission's Complaints Jurisdiction

The Commission's jurisdiction to investigate complaints is set out in Section 120(1)(b) of the Mental Health Act 1983. This section of the Act defines two types of complaint which are within the remit of the Commission's investigative powers: any complaint made by a person in respect of a matter that occurred while he *was* detained under this Act and which he finds has not been satisfactorily dealt with by the Managers; and any other complaint as to the exercise of powers or discharge of duties conferred or imposed by the Act in respect of a person who is or has been detained.

The Commission's Third Biennial Report detailed how at that time the Commission received and handled complaints. The report also made mention of the Commission's intention to strive for improvement in its performance in handling complaints. It was noted that there had been occasional complaints to the Commission about the length of time taken to complete complaint investigations, and also about failures to notify complainants about the outcome. Since then, the Commission has centralised its administration in Nottingham and has developed a standard Policy, Procedure and Guidelines for handling complaints, which has recently been put into operation. Further reference to this is made below.

5.2 Complaints statistics

In the period 1st July 1989 to 30th June 1990 the Commission received 1068 complaints, 458 of these being judged worthy of pursuit by two Commissioners. These figures compare with 1003 complaints received in the preceding Biennial Report period 1989-1991. A breakdown of the complaints received is set out in table 1. Column one, sets out the total number of complaints divided into the broad categories indicated while column two indicates the number of complaints followed up by two Commissioners.

5.3 The Commission's investigation of complaints and centralisation

The centralisation of the Commission's administration prompted the development of a Complaints Policy, Procedure and Guidelines to be used in the investigation of all complaints by the Commission. The policy can be found at Appendix 5. The benefits of the policy are two-fold:

a. it enables all complaints to be dealt with consistently;

b. it provides a basis for formal training of Commissioners and Commission staff who are responsible for handling complaints.

One of the major new features of the policy is the inclusion of time limits. It is the Commission's intention that most complaint investigations will be completed within 14 weeks. This will not always be possible and the policy emphasizes the importance of not sacrificing the quality of an investigation in order to comply with the time limits. The policy also places appropriate emphasis on keeping complainants informed of the progress and outcome of a complaints investigation. In the past the Commission has been correctly criticised for not always doing this. The Complaints NSC has overall responsibility for monitoring the Commission's undertaking of its complaints jurisdiction, both in terms of quality and time limits, and they will be doing so on a regular basis.

In January 1991 the Commission held its first training session for complaints convenors and relevant Commission staff, and it was particularly useful to have a contribution from the Deputy Health Service Commissioner, Mr Oswald, on the investigation of complaints generally. A further training session was held in June.

The implementation of the new policy has caused the Commission to review its ability to carry out its complaints jurisdiction within its present structure and administrative resources. Whilst Commission staff are responsible for providing administrative support for the undertaking of this aspect of the Commission's statutory responsibilities, the burden of carrying out complaints investigations falls on Commissioners. Commissioners are part time and, apart from the limited training initiatives undertaken by the Commission itself, are untrained in the investigation of complaints. This situation compares unfavourably with complaints bodies such as the Health Service Commissioner or the local authority ombudsman, whose sole activity is the investigation of complaints, a task which is undertaken by full-time staff. As a consequence it is undoubtedly true that at times it is a major challenge for Commissioners to deal with complaints to the standard set by the Commission. The Commission is a health authority and in accordance with the Hospital Complaints Procedure Act has established a policy and procedure for complaints made against Commissioners. Although there are very few in number it is important that the Commission deals with them properly and a copy of the policy can be found at Annex 6.

5.4 The Health Service Commissioner

In the third Biennial Report (page 18) the Commission indicated its concern that the Health Service Commissioner is forbidden by statute from sharing information on those cases involving detained patients. Although this remains a problem, the Commission has had very useful contacts with the office of the Health Service Commissioner, including a valuable meeting between the Commission Chair and the Health Service Commissioner. One important issue resolved is which body should first look into complaints from or on behalf of detained patients. The following agreement was reached:

a. where a complaint from a detained patient is exclusively, or primarily, about the circumstances or consequences of detention, the Mental Health Act Commission should intervene first;

b. where a complaint from a detained patient is about matters not concerned with the circumstances or consequences of detention, the Health Service Commissioner should carry out an investigation (subject always to the normal screening process whereby the Health Service Commissioner decides whether or not to investigate);

c. where a complaint concerns matters potentially within the jurisdiction of both bodies, the complainant should be advised first to approach the Mental Health Act Commission.

During the period under review the Commission has collaborated with the Local Authority Ombudsman in the investigation of one particular case.

The Commission has also had involvement in a complaint concerning a General Practitioner who allegedly refused to attend to make an urgent assessment under the provisions of the Act on the grounds that the doctor had no previous knowledge of the patient. This case highlighted some difficulties in the Commission's relationship with Family Health Service Authorities and is set out in full in Case 2.

5.5 Complaints procedures in the Special Hospitals

The first two biennial reports of the Commission expressed profound anxieties about the manner in which patients' complaints in the Special Hospitals are dealt with, and the absence of a uniform agreed complaints policy for the three Special Hospitals. The Third Biennial Report critically commented on a nationally agreed complaints policy for the Special Hospitals, which the Commission was advised was issued by the Department of Health in May 1989. During the period under review the Commission has continued to pursue vigorously with the SHSA the need for an adequate complaints policy. The SHSA is to be congratulated on the importance they obviously attach to this matter. At the beginning of 1991 the SHSA issued a complaints statement of policy which takes into account many of the Commission's criticisms and concerns. Procedures to implement the policy are being developed and the Commission will be commenting upon these. The existence of an acceptable statement of policy does not in itself mean that the increased problems surrounding the investigation of complaints in the Special Hospitals have been or will be overcome. A complaints policy will be successful only if it is operated within an ethos that accept that patients have a right to have express legitimate complaints and that the receipt and proper investigation of such complaints is an essential contribution to how well each Special Hospital assesses what it is doing and maintains standards. There is clearly a long way to go before such an ethos is established throughout the Special Hospitals. The Commission is much encouraged by the commitment shown by the SHSA, hospital management teams and many members of staff to achieving this objective.

5.6 Complaints Investigated during the Last Two Years

The complaints investigated in the period under review have continued to be a mixture of the serious and those which some might characterise as more trivial, but which may, nevertheless, still be of vital importance to the complainant. As in previous biennial reports this part of the chapter identifies, by reference to the Commission's complaints categories, some complaints which highlight the issues they raise and sets out some of the difficulties experienced by Commissioners when undertaking their statutory responsibility to investigate complaints.

(a) Category A — offences against the person

This has continued to be one of the most significant categories of complaints received by the Commission.

It remains Commission policy that allegations of assault on patients should result in a visit to the hospital concerned by two Commissioners within 24 hours. Where the alleged assault did not occur recently there is now a discretion not to arrange an immediate visit where it is appropriate. The purpose of the Commission visits is to:

  i. ensure that any relevant medical evidence is secure; and

ii. ensure that the hospital or nursing home management are taking appropriate action, including where necessary involvement of the police. These authorities are in the main much better equipped to investigate complaints and in such circumstances the Commission's primary responsibility is to ensure that the allegations are thoroughly investigated.

The Commission does, however, on occasion become indirectly involved in looking into such complaints. One such involved an allegation that a patient had been dragged across the floor by her hair and called names. This mistreatment was alleged to have resulted in her suffering carpet burns on the knees. The Commission reviewed all the relevant documentation. It has been noted by the RMO that she had sustained grazes on both knees and bruises on her left shin which, in the view of the medical officer, were consistent with the patient's kicking and knocking on a door whilst in a disturbed state. For very understandable reasons the complaint was brought to the Commission's attention by the patient quite some time after the event and such delay frequently makes it very hard to investigate allegations properly.

Taking into account all the written evidence that was available, Commissioners concluded that the patient had been restrained physically, possibly with force being used, but it could not be shown that undue or improper force had been used.

Although many complaints in this category remain unresolved, it remains crucial that complaints are investigated promptly and thoroughly. One major criticism of the manner in which such complaints have been investigated in the Special Hospitals relates to the practice of referring serious allegations to the police on the undertaking that, even where appropriate no parallel management enquiries would be undertaken. The Commission warmly welcomes the provision in the SHSA's complaints statement and policy, which require such managements investigations where appropriate.

(b) Category B — medical care and services

This is a common complaint category which is often combined with complaints about other aspects about which dissatisfaction is felt. Commission action on this aspect of the complaint is usually to encourage the patient to discuss any particular problems with the doctors or nurses involved. The Commission will help the patient to do this, if necessary. Other aspects of the complaint will be referred to the hospital managers and the Commission will follow-up and take the necessary action to ensure that the matter has been properly investigated.

(c) Category C — Medical treatment

A high proportion of complaints in this category reflect concerns, distress and resentment by patients about having to accept psychotropic medication against their will. On investigation there are few cases where RMO's or their deputies are found to have exceeded their powers under Section 58. However, the review of patient's records all too often show poor organisation of medication cards, consent forms and second opinion doctor recommendations, resulting in uncertainty for the ward staff who actually supervise the administration of the drugs. In such situations the patient's poor comprehension and reluctance to co-operate are all too understandable.

In one particular instance it was reported that there had been several changes in junior doctor within 16 months. This resulted in the patients medication not being checked or altered despite a recommendation in the case of one particular patient that this should be done. The Commission included a mention of this situation in its report back letter to the hospital, and will continue to check on the steps taken to improve the situation.

The Commission's response to most complaints about medical treatment is to encourage the patient to discuss their worries with the RMO and to advise the patients about their rights in respect of a Mental Health Review Tribunal and the safeguards under Part IV of the Act.

The Commission still remains extremely concerned about the apparent lack of knowledge amongst doctors and other health professionals about the consent to treatment provisions in the Mental Health Act.

(d) Category F — Domestic care, living arrangements and privacy

Complaints in this category are fairly common, particularly from long stay patients.

For example as the result of one complaint letter Commissioners decided to carry out an unannounced visit to a hospital which resulted in a report which was highly critical of the ward. In a matter of weeks the ward was emptied and patients moved to a newly decorated empty ward which, although not ideal, was a considerable improvement.

In another case, hospital managers gave a positive response which detailed steps which they were to take to rectify poor decor and facilities at the unit in question.

(e) Category G — Finance, benefits and property

The increased use of the private sector for the care of detained patients has given rise to some incidental problems about payment for hospitalisation. In most cases the hospital concerned and the doctors entitled to payment for provision of their medical services will ensure that the patient is covered by adequate insurance or that other financial resources (for example a relative is willing to pay) are available. The Commission has begun to receive a few complaints where there was no such clarification and the ensuing argument about financial responsibility has been detrimental to the patient's health.

The Commission has also begun to receive some complaints concerning the admission of patients to private facilities when health service facilities were available, but possible admission to them not explored.

On one particular complaint, a patient detained in a private hospital, who, at a Mental Health Review Tribunal hearing, indicated a wish to be treated in a NHS hospital — a wish that was specifically referred to in the Tribunal's decision — the patient nevertheless remained detained in the private hospital.

Such complaints frequently raise very complex issues of professional responsibilities, attention to private care and contractual liability for payment of hospital fees. The Commission anticipates that the number of such complaints will continue to increase, and it will continue to monitor them carefully and if necessary issue guidance.

(f) Category H — Deprivation of liberty

Complaints in this category often relate to the manner in which the person was detained rather than to the fact of their detention. In many of the cases problems have arisen when S135 or 136 has been used, particularly where the mental health services and the police and individuals involved are unclear about the procedures to be used, although it is important to note that complaints about the role of the police in mental health matters are relatively few. Section 136 empowers a police officer to remove a mentally disordered person from a public place to a place of safety, usually a police station or a hospital.

One complaint, however, did involve the police, although it eventually reflected inactivity by the mental health service. In one area extensive local concerns were expressed about police policies and procedures which resulted in extensive use of S136 without subsequent involvement of Approved Social Workers (ASWs) and doctors who had knowledge of the patients concerned or specialised psychiatric skills. These practices had been reinforced by a local scarcity of ASWs and S12 approved doctors. After extended local deliberation, a new inter-agency policy was drafted. A pilot scheme was introduced into one police division which involved ASWs in initial screening of all arrested persons showing signs of mental disorder and of disturbed individuals found by police in public places.

The Commission visiting team for the locality has been kept informed of these developments and has commented on the draft procedures involved and it is hoped that it will result in the proper and efficient implementation of Section 136.

(g) Category J — Leave, parole, transfer and other absences from hospital

The majority of complaints in this category still involve delays in the transfer of patients from the Special Hospitals; this topic has been addressed in greater detail elsewhere in the report (see page 21).

Other problems often relate to difficulties or uncertainties arising out of the use of S17, which enables an RMO to grant leave to a detained patient with or without an escort for periods ranging from a very short time to a number of weeks. The decision to grant leave rests with the RMO who cannot delegate this power to another professional.

In one instance a patient's father complained that his son should not have been allowed to go on leave because of his mental state. It was established that the RMO had spoken to the patient and had agreed that he could go home for a change of clothes, unescorted and should return by noon. The precise details of the decision were not adequately relayed to the nursing staff and the patient's nearest relative (who was his father) was not informed. No check was made to see if the patient had keys, money, or whether someone would be at home. The nursing notes merely recorded that the patient was on leave for a few hours. During the evening the patients father arrived on the ward to see his son. The ward staff were unaware of the patients whereabouts. The patient's father filled in a 'missing person' form and the police were notified. The RMO was informed the following day that the patient had died the previous day. This complaint highlights the importance of ensuring that clear instructions are given by RMOs to nursing staff when using Section 17 to grant leave and that the conditions attached by the RMO to the granting of leave are fully recorded. As a consequence of the Commission's findings in this complaint Section 17 procedures were revised.

(h) Category M — administration

Many complaints in this category relate to delays or other difficulties in processing appeals by patients to the hospital management for discharge. One important factor has been the changes in health authority membership consequent upon implementation of the NHS and Community Care Act. The Health Authorities remain the Mental Health Act managers, although they are entitled to appoint a sub-committee composed entirely of non-health authority members to carry out the management functions. Many authorities were confused by the new arrangements as they related to the undertaking of the Mental Health Act manager's function and the Commission has received various requests for advice on that matter.

There are still, as recorded in the previous report, a number of complaints which relate to lack of information given to the patient or to the nearest relative. In one such case the patients parents complained that they received insufficient information about their son's care after his admission to hospital, despite the fact that the patient has no objection to their involvement. The Commission upheld the complaint that they were not consulted or informed about the granting of leave of absence, nor did they have the opportunity to discuss with the clinical team that treatment plan which was agreed in the first few days of his admission.

(i) Category N — Local authority services and functions

The complaints in this category generally relate to the inadequate range of appropriate facilities, which often means that the recommendations of Mental Health Review Tribunals cannot be met.

(j) Category P — Ethnic, cultural and religious matters

Complaints related wholly or partially to racial or ethnic discrimination are relatively infrequent, but they do present some serious problems which can be difficult to reconcile to the complainants' and other parties' satisfaction. This is particularly the case where the complaint relates to lack of special facilities or awareness of staff in hospital environments which are poorly adapted for the practice of modern psychiatry let alone of meeting the subtleties of individual patients needs.

In some instances irreconcilable differences of expectations are apparent, in which despite the best efforts of staff, special needs are not met. For example the family of a young black man complained that his behaviour in a secure unit was being controlled solely by excessive medication and that no psychotherapy had been offered to him. On investigation it transpired that dosages were greatly in excess of BNF recommended levels, but that even so the unit had been unable to cope with the patients violent outbursts. It was apparent that his substantial physical size and behaviour had warranted greatly increased doses, which had been approved by a Second Opinion Appointed Doctor, and that other forms of therapy had been attempted, but with little effect.

In the event the patient's behaviour improved when he was transferred to another secure facility where staffing numbers and special skills in management of disturbed behaviour enabled medication levels to be reduced progressively.

The rarity of complaints specifying recial discrimination has not convinced the Commission that this is not a problem within the mental health system. The racist nature of a person's behaviour is often difficult to prove and patients making complaints with a racist connotation may not specify racism as the complaint. Some Commissioners have observed that black patients tend to regard racist attitudes of staff as a normal experience of institutional life that does not qualify as a matter for complaint.

(k) Category Q — Department of Health, Home Office and other Government Departments

Although not very common, complaints in this category generally relate to alleged Home Office delays in matters relating to restricted patients or problems of liaison between various involved bodies (the hospital, police, etc).

In one instance a three month interval had elapsed between the Home Office warrant for recall and its implementation. The Home Office warrant dated 20 September 1990 had an accompanying letter which did not mention the possibility of police involvement. The patients readmission did not occur until 28 December 1990 following a violent incident that took place during one of the patient's visits to the hospital. Commissioners felt that if the warrant had been acted on immediately his earlier return to hospital might have forestalled the severe breakdown which the patient suffered at the end of the year. The Commission's involvement resulted in a change of Home Office procedures.

(l) Category R — Complaints about the Mental Health Act Commission

These are still very few in number and are usually about delays in notifying complainants of the outcome of the investigation. The Commission's new policy and procedures will hopefully result in the eradication of such complaints.

Table 1

Category	No of complaints	% of total complaints	No followed up 2 commissioners	% of category followed up	% of total followed up
A. Offences against the person	106	9.9	66	62.3	14.4
B. Medical care and services	63	5.8	25	39.7	5.5
C. Medical treatment	218	20.4	54	27.8	11.8
D. Nursing care and services	90	8.4	44	48.9	9.6
E. Other professional care and services	38	3.6	20	52.6	4.3
F. Domestic care, living arrangements privacy	49	4.6	22	44.9	4.7
G. Finance, benefits property	51	4.8	30	58.8	6.6
H. Deprivation of liberty	138	12.9	37	26.8	8.1
J. Leave, parole, transfer and other absences from hospital	143	13.4	90	62.9	19.7
K. Mental health review tribunal matters	54	5.2	19	35.2	4.1
L. Family matters	17	1.6	10	58.8	2.2
M. Administration	40	3.7	14	35.0	3.1
N. Local authority services/functions	11	1.0	6	54.5	1.3
O. Social educational, recreational matters	12	1.1	8	66.6	1.7
P. Ethnic cultural religious matters	7	0.7	4	57.1	0.9
Q. DofH, Home Office, other government departments	13	1.2	3	23.1	0.7
R. Mental health act commission	1	0.1	0	0	0
S. Others	17	1.6	6	35.3	1.3
Totals	1068	100%	458	42.9%	100%

6.
CONSENT TO TREATMENT AND SECOND OPINIONS

6.1 Introduction

The administration and monitoring of Part IV of the Mental Health Act continues to be one of the most important activities of the Commission. Section 57 applies to psychosurgery and the surgical implantation of hormones for the suppression of male sexual drive. The safeguards under this section apply both to formal and informal patients. Section 58 applies to electroconvulsive therapy (ECT) and the administration of medication for mental disorder after three months since the first occasion in the period of detention when medicines were administered. These safeguards apply to most detained patients.

6.2 Section 57

All referrals of patients to the Commission under Section 57 were in relation to psychosurgery. There were no referrals in relation to hormone implantation. The majority of psychosurgery operations continue to be undertaken in the Geoffrey Knight Unit at the Brook Hospital in London. The numbers referred under Section 57 fluctuate considerably in part due to the changing availability of Yttrium rods which are used in the operations.

The total numbers of patients referred to the Commission in the period under review (1.7.89-30.6.91) was 65. This is an increase in the numbers identified in previous biennial reports which were:

1983-5	57
1985-7	54
1987-9	52

Certificates were issued for 56 patients. In one case the certificate was withheld because the person was unable to consent. The remaining eight referrals were either cancelled or constitute current cases.

The centres specialising in the work covered by Section 57 are:

Brook Hospital	45
Priory Hospital	7
Atkinson Morley Hospital	3
Pinderfields Hospital	1
Total operations	56

Gender of referrals:

Male	20
Female	45
Total	65

Under the new centralised administration of the Commission, the Commission's responsibilities in relation to Section 57 are overseen by the NSC on Consent. A group of six Commissioners supported by administrative staff is responsible for processing referrals, arranging visits, and collating the reports required under Section 61.

The New Procedure

The Commission is sensitive to the fact that a referral for psychosurgery comes at the end of prolonged efforts to alleviate suffering by extensive courses of treatment and that the patient has usually been ill for a very long time. Every effort is made to ensure that patients are visited in their local hospital and in familiar surroundings but this is only possible for patients who are living in the British Isles. When patients are referred from other countries they are usually visited at the centre where the operation is to be carried out. Furthermore, many patients are not resident in hospital at the time of referral and consequently it is not always easy for the referring doctor to arrange for the two other professionals (one a nurse) "professionally concerned with the patient's medical treatment" to meet the visiting team. Nevertheless, the Commission appointees cannot provide a certificate under Section 57 unless they have been able to consult with the two other professionals. This is even more problematic when the patient has come from another country. The RMO in such a case is usually the Specialist Psychiatrist attached to the unit where the operation is to take place. The two other professionals are drawn from the same unit though they may only have known the person for a week or less.

To ensure that the referral procedure is carried out efficiently and to minimise some of the difficulties, a new procedure has recently been agreed by the Commission.

When the RMO, or the unit where the operation is to take place (as in the case of patients from abroad) contacts the Commission, a doctor is appointed who will carry out the first part of the procedure within two months of the proposed date of the operation. The appointed doctor will discuss with the patient's consultant psychiatrist the proposals for psychosurgery and may visit. There may be reasons why the appointed doctor will advise against proceeding to the second stage. It sometimes happens that further treatment recommended by the specialist psychiatrist has not yet begun and the visiting doctor may advise waiting until such further treatments have been completed. Otherwise the doctor accompanied by non medical appointees will visit the patient within six weeks prior to the proposed operation and consult the relevant professionals. If all three decide to certify under sub-section 2 of Section 57 (2) and the appointed doctor decides to certify under sub-section (b) of the same section, then the certification will be notified immediately to those concerned and subsequently the certificate sent to the Commission office.

6.3 Section 58

In the period under review the overall number of second opinions has declined from the 7592 recorded in the previous two years to 7169. There has been no substantial change in the distribution of second opinions by sex, type of treatment of Section authorising detention (see Tables on pages . . .).

(a) Centralisation

Centralisation has enabled a single national service to be established for the implementation of Section 58. The administrative arrangements for the new service maintain a close relationship between the visits of the Second Opinion Appointed Doctors (SOADs) and the support provided for the Commission Visiting Teams. The Commission staff are developing effective working relationships with the hospitals in their areas and with the Section 58 Appointed Doctors who make themselves available to visit, often at very short notice.

(b) Monitoring

A single system is now in operation for monitoring the reports received by the Commission under Sections 58 and

61 of the Act. For this purpose the members of the Consent to Treatment NSC work in three multi-disciplinary groups which meet every three months. The monitoring groups include seven medical members of the Commission, all of whom are experienced Section 58 Appointed Doctors.

(c) Recommended dose ranges and the British National Formulary (BNF)

The monitoring group reviews reports authorising compulsory treatments with higher than usual doses of medication and long courses of ECT (above twelve treatments) with particular care, but the Commission itself does not set any arbitrary limit to treatment, this being entirely a matter for the professional judgement of the patient's RMO and the Appointed Doctor.

(d) Agreement between Section 58 Appointed Doctor and the RMO

There remains a high degree of concordance between the treatment plan proposed by the RMO and the treatment authorised by the Second Opinion Appointed Doctors, though when failure to agree after negotiation does occur this causes considerable difficulty, especially for the clinical team responsible for the continuing care of the patient. A revised report form to provide data on the extent to which treatment plans are modified in the light of discussions between the RMO and Section 58 Appointed Doctor is to be introduced to allow the Commission to assess the contribution made by SOADs to clinical treatment decisions.

(e) Ethnic monitoring

The new SOAD report form being prepared will also include data on the ethnic category of detained patients for whom compulsory treatment under the provisions of Section 58 (3) (b) is requested.

6.4 Section 61 (Review of Treatment)

There is still some misunderstanding about the Commission's requirements of hospitals under Section 61. Whereas some hospitals have been submitting reports regularly every few months, other hospitals have forwarded very few reports on forms MHAC 1. Hospital Managers should ensure that MHAC 1 forms are completed and returned to the Commission at the beginning of every period of renewable detention and to furnish additional reports if requested by the SOAD. Patients under restriction order must have a review of treatment reported on MHAC 1 annually when a report is sent to the Home Office. In addition hospitals are asked to inform the Commission when a detained patient receiving treatment on the authority of a form 39 is discharged or consents to treatment. Hospitals are advised to institute a system at ward level for monitoring the cancellation or changes of form 38 and form 39 since at present ward records are often found to be unclear as to the current consenting status of the patient.

6.5 Section 62 and Emergency Treatment

It is not always clear in the records whether emergency treatment for mental disorder is being given under the provisions of common law or with the patient's consent or under the provisions of Section 62. Furthermore it is not always understood that treatment administered during the short term sections is not covered by the provisions of Section 62. Patients have been held under Section 5(2) or admitted under Section 4 specifically so that emergency treatment can be given on the assumption that Section 62 applies. There is a need for managers, medical staff and

Social Services Departments to be aware that this is not permissible and of the limitations of common law in relation to emergency treatment so that early arrangements can be made to consider admission under Section 2 or 3 when continuation of treatment without consent is necessary. Similar problems arise in relation to the administration of 'as required' or 'PRN' medication as this is frequently not incorporated in either the consent certified by the RMO or the authorisation provided by the Appointed Doctor.

6.6 Introduction of the Code of Practice

The detailed guidance given in the Code of Practice on arrangements for Second Opinion Appointed Doctor (SOAD) visits, the description of the treatment plan and the review requirements required by the Act have proved to be of assistance. Some modification may be necessary; for example, the scrutiny of prime copies of the statutory documents by Appointed Doctors has been found to be largely impracticable and clearer advice needs to be given that consent to treatment forms should always define an upper limit to the medication being proposed.

6.7 Nurses and the Consent to Treatment Provisions

Many nurses are still not fully aware of the legal significance of Forms 38 and 39. It needs to be emphasised that it is *their* professional responsibility, before administering medication, to ensure that the appropriate form is correctly completed and that the medication listed on the Form 38/39 is the same as the patient's prescription sheet. Where there is a discrepancy the nurse must contact the patient's RMO or his/her deputy to rectify the problem.

Chapter 16 (Medical Treatment and Second Opinions) in the Code of Practice gives guidance on matters relating to giving of medication.

6.8 Statutory Consultees

SOADs often have difficulties in identifying and locating a third person who is 'professionally involved with the patient'. As well as consulting with the RMO and nurse, the Appointed Doctor has to consult with a third professional in order to comply with the Mental Health Act. If a third professional who has been acquainted with the patient cannot be identified, the Appointed Doctor is unable to complete the certification.

Hospital staff should be aware of the range of people who may be consulted. In addition to social workers, occupational therapists and psychologists, there are also physiotherapists, chaplains, pharmacists, dieticians and speech therapists who may be involved. However, the continuing difficulties are related more to the organisation and timing of the visit, and to a lack of forward planning by the RMO. This is especially true in hospitals which rarely use Section 58. When such difficulties are identified by Appointed Doctors on the report form they are drawn to the attention of the visiting teams for the hospital concerned and followed up by them.

6.9 Out-of-Hours Service

It has been suggested that administrative arrangements should be made to receive and act upon requests for Second Opinions under the Act outside usual working hours, at weekends and bank holidays. At present the Commission believes the cost of establishing a full emergency service cannot be justified by the small demand. RMOs begin treatment under Section 62 in these circumstances. However, a system for providing more direct support to clinicians when making emergency requests out of hours is being considered.

6.10 Detained Patients on Extended Leave

Requests for SOADs to visit patients at home or in Day Hospitals are occasionally received when the patient is continuing on treatment while on extended leave under the provisions of Section 17. This is particularly likely to arise in relation to patients with long term mental illness in sheltered accommodation which is not a registered mental nursing home. The Code of Practice (Para. 20.8) points out that the provisions of Part IV of the Act continue to apply to patients granted leave under Section 17 but also advises that "If it becomes necessary to administer treatment in the absence of the patient's consent under Part IV, the patient should be recalled to hospital". However, it would be disruptive to recall incapable patients to hospital when they are continuing on treatment initially administered on the authority of the RMO, merely because the three months period has elapsed and further treatment requires the certification provided by the Second Opinion Doctor under Section 58. Nevertheless, the organisation of Second Opinion visits in community settings presents many practical difficulties e.g. in scrutinising documents and identifying a suitable third professional, and is likely to remain exceptional. However, leave of absence may only be revoked under Section 17(4) and the patient recalled to hospital when it is necessary in the interests of his health or safety or for the protection of other persons that he again becomes an inpatient. It may therefore be unlawful to resolve leave and recall a patient solely for the administration of treatment without consent or for the procedures under Section 58 to be carried out.

6.11 Treatment Plans

Treatment plans for medication which are recorded in unnecessarily specific terms on the statutory forms continue to present difficulties, in spite of the advice given within the Code of Practice which allows for some flexibility in the description of the treatment. Minor adjustments in the prescribed treatment are often made without the statutory consent forms being up-dated, invalidating the certificate of consent or authorisation on Form 39. This is the most frequent cause of discrepancies between the treatment plan described under Part IV and the actual treatment which the patient is receiving.

6.12 Criteria for Determining Consent

The 'Witham Case' (see chapter 11) raised concerns about the correct interpretation of the capacity and consent provisions in both Sections 57 and 58. When considering whether a patient is consenting, the Commission ensures that the patient understands the nature, purpose and likely effect of the treatment proposed. The Witham judgment appeared to suggest that consent rests not on actual understanding but simply on the patient's intellectual capacity to understand and agree to the treatment proposed. The Commission has taken legal advice on this approach and advised all SOAD appointed person to continue with their approach of requiring both a capacity to consent and adequate understanding of the treatment and its consequences.

6.13 Appointment and training of SOADs

A revised procedure for the appointment of Section 58 Appointed Doctors is being implemented. The Commission is intending shortly to review its method of selection of registered medical practitioners to be SOADs. Seminars for Section 58 Appointed Doctors have been re-established and a new edition of the SOAD newsletter has been issued.

6.14 NHS Indemnity for SOADs

The recent changes in the indemnity arrangements for NHS doctors required the Commission to rectify the indemnity arrangements for SOADs. All SOADs are now indemnified by the Commission in the same way as NHS doctors.

6.15 Legal Duties under the SOAD System

The Witham case has provided the Commission with a welcome opportunity to seek clarification of the legal relationship between the Commission and appointed persons and doctors under Part IV of the Act.

The Commission performs, on behalf of the Secretary of State, the statutory function of appointing a registered medical practitioner — and other non-medical persons in Section 57 cases — for the purpose of providing a second opinion — and in Section 57 cases of verifying consent — under the 'consent to treatment' provisions of the Act. The persons appointed may or may not be members of the Commission. Recently the Commission abandoned its earlier policy of appointing only Commission members for Section 57 cases. In discharging this responsibility to appoint medical practitioners and other persons the Commission is discharging a public law function. As such the Court determined that it is amenable to supervision by the courts, but it incurs no liability to compensation for breach of its statutory duty. Any breach leads only to a questioning of any decision by the Commission in making an appointment.

Once the Commission has made its appointment for the particular second opinion — and verified consent in Section 57 cases — it is left exclusively to the appointed persons and doctors to carry out their responsibility for the actions and decisions of the appointees. They are neither servants nor agents of the Commission, they act in their individual capacities and are responsible for their own actions. The Commission also does not act as an appeal body against any decision made by the second opinion doctor, or other persons in a Section 57 case if a certificate is refused; the only remedy is a challenge by way of a judicial review.

While the second opinion doctor applies his or her clinical judgment to the appropriateness of the treatment prescribed by the RMO, no relationship is established between the doctor and the patient such as to create any legal liability in private law. For example, in Section 58 cases the law regards the second opinion doctor as performing an administrative act of issuing or denying a certificate that prescribed medication or ECT may be administered. The decision of the Court in the "Witham" case is the subject of an appeal.

6.16 Specialisation within Psychiatry

Occasionally it is suggested that a SOAD should be drawn from the sub-speciality applicable to the patient, for example when compulsory treatment proposed is for an elderly person with depression or a person with severe mental impairment. It is a tribute to the breadth of experience of the Section 58 Appointed Doctors that this rarely presents a problem, but it is open to any SOAD not to undertake a visit if the request suggests that a more specialised opinion than they can provide is required. Some Section 58 Appointed Doctors have indicated that they do not wish at present to be involved in the authorisation of compulsory treatment with Clozapine as their experience with this drug remains limited. Steps have been taken to ensure that Section 58 Appointed Doctors are informed before the visit if the treatment plan proposed includes Clozapine so that appropriate arrangements can be made.

6.17 Clozapine (Clozaril — Sandoz)

Clozapine (Clozaril) has recently emerged as an oral anti-psychotic, licensed for use in schizophrenia resistant to other anti-psychotics. In 1989 Clozapine was made available for use in treatment-resistant patients under strictly controlled haematological monitoring. The Consent to Treatment NSC has considered the status of Clozapine. It has taken note of the fact that this oral anti-psychotic is being increasingly used in patients with schizophrenia resistant to other treatments. There are some patients who will agree to take the tablets but who are unable to give valid consent or who refuse to agree to the regular blood samples required for the treatment. When considering Clozapine treatment the RMO and the SOAD must consider the possible adverse effects of the monitoring procedures. Authority to administer Clozapine will include the authority to secure the necessary samples for monitoring, though whether the RMO will wish to continue to exercise this authority if the patient maintains a refusal to consent and to co-operate must be a clinical judgment made by the RMO in the individual case.

6.18 Consent to Treatment and Life Threatening Disorders

The Commission has been asked for its views about the use of the Mental Health Act in the treatment of severe anorexia nervosa. It is the Commission's opinion that anorexia nervosa falls within the definition of mental disorder in the Act and therefore treatment of anorexia nervosa necessary for the health or safety of the patient, including involuntary feeding and maintenance of hydration, is permissible in patients whose anorexia is causing serious concern. It will remain a matter of sensitive judgment on the part of clinicians and approved social workers at what stage or level of severity of disorder a compulsory treatment order should be sought.

6.19 The Compulsory Treatment of Children and Young People

The Commission is aware of the problems caused by the lack of clarity of the legal position relating to the compulsory treatment of children and young people and in particular those under the age of sixteen. The recent judgment of the Court of Appeal in the case of re 'R' (Court of Appeal 1991) will be the subject of further Commission consideration, particularly in relation to its implications for the guidance given in the Mental Health Act Code of Practice.

Statistical information

Section 58

Table 1a: Totals by gender

Male	3048	42.5%
Female	4121	57.2%
Total	7169	100%

Table 1b: Totals by type of treatment

Medicines	3023	42.2
ECT	3978	57.5
Both	166	2.5
Total	7169	100%

Table 1c: Totals by section authorising detention

S2 (assessment)	872	12.1%
S3 (treatment)	5471	76.3%
S37 (Hospital Order)	585	8.2%
Others	241	3.4%
Total	7169	100%

Table 2: Totals by Health Region and Diagnosis

Health region	Mental illness	Mental impairment	Psychopathic disorder	
Mersey	260	5	1	266
North West	727	12	—	739
West Midlands	637	6	3	646
Wales	354	3	—	357
Oxford	246	39	2	287
NW Thames	329	33	6	368
NE Thames	396	5	2	403
East Anglia	304	10	—	314
South Western	453	9	—	462
Wessex	281	4	1	286
SW Thames	186	5	—	191
SE Thames	337	1	—	338
Northern	316	21	1	338
Yorkshire	516	19	1	533
Trent	646	8	—	654
Private Mental Nursing Homes	254	39	14	307
Broadmoor Special Hosp	153	—	9	162
Rampton Special Hosp	166	90	22	278
Ashworth Special Hosp	181	27	21	229
Special Health Authority	91	9	—	100
Total	6830	345	83	7258

Table 3: MHA category totals

		%
Mental Illness	6830	94.1
Mental Impairment	345	4.8
Psychopathic Disorder	83	1.1
Total	7258	100

Table 4: Treatment by gender in mental illness category

	Female No	%	Male No	%
ECT	2827	71.1	1134	39.7
Medicine	1040	26.2	1671	58.5
Both	105	2.7	53	1.8
Total	3972		2858	6830

7.
THE REVIEW OF DECISIONS TO WITHHOLD PATIENTS' MAIL

The Commission has a statutory duty under section 121(7) to review decisions at the Special Hospitals to withhold postal packets or anything contained in them. The Managers of a Special Hospital may withhold outgoing mail if they consider that the postal packet is likely to cause distress to the addressee or anyone else (other than a member of the hospital staff) or is likely to cause danger to any person. These decisions are subject to review by the Commision at the request of the patient. If the addressee has made a written request to the RMO, the Managers or the Secretary of State that mail from any detained patient be not forwarded, the withholding of mail is not subject to review. This applies both to patients detained under the Act in Special Hospitals and in other hospitals. Incoming mail may be withheld from a Special Hospital patient if, in the opinion of the Managers, it is necessary to do so in the interests of the safety of the patient or for the protection of other persons. Such decisions may be reviewed by the Commission at the request of the patient or the person who sent the packet. The Commission has a power to direct that the item of mail or any part of its contents should not be withheld. The Commission's procedure in relation to this statutory responsibility can be found at Appendix 4.

During the period under review the Commission received six requests for review. In five cases it was decided that the packages withheld be released and in one case the hospital decision was upheld in part.

8.
THE MENTAL HEALTH ACT CODE OF PRACTICE

The Code of Practice was laid before Parliament in the Autumn of 1989. The Code has been printed in pocket size edition with a distinctive blue cover in order to encourage its regular use by every practitioner and administrator. There has been considerable interest in the Code and the initial demand for copies caused some delay in their availability. Further reprints have now been published.

At the beginning of 1990 the Secretary of State asked the Commission to undertake two tasks:

a. To monitor the implementation of the Code of Practice and advise Ministers from time to time on any changes to the Code which the Commission thinks appropriate.

b. To consider and then advise Ministers on three detailed criticisms of the Code raised by Lord Mottistone in the House of Lords debate on the Code (on 29 January 1990)

The latter task has been completed.

The Commission warmly welcomed the Secretary of State's request to monitor the implementation of the Code, in particular because the request is an indicator that the Code of Practice may be amended from time to time to reflect ever changing best practice. The Commission has appointed a National Standing Committee to monitor the Code.

As soon as the Code became widely available, members of the Commission visiting Hospitals and Mental Nursing Homes and meeting with Social Services Departments, made the Code of Practice one of the issues that is always addressed.

Initially, particular attention was paid to the Code's availability and distribution and mental health professionals were encouraged to use it in their work, and as a training aid. Members of the Commission were, and continue to be, concerned about its easy availability to patients, their relatives and supporters.

As familiarity with the Code has developed, Commissioners have been concentrating on ensuring that providers of mental health care produce policies in relation to those issues identified as requiring them in the Code and they are also undertaking a more detailed examination of its implementation.

Much progress has been made in many areas with implementation of the Code. For example, Somerset Health Authority has made good use of the code as a basis for training sessions.

9.
SERVICES FOR DIFFICULT AND OFFENDER PATIENTS

9.1 Introduction

The Second and Third Biennial Reports expressed particular concern with services for this category of patients. In the period covered by the present report there has been much public discussion and criticism of how mentally disordered offenders are dealt with by the health and criminal justice systems. The Commission welcomes two recent initiatives. First, the issue of a Home Office guidance circular (66/90) on the existing provisions, and second, the announcement in November 1990 of the institution by the Department of Health and the Home Office of a review of services for mentally disordered offenders under the chairmanship of Dr John Reed. It has become increasingly apparent, from reports of delays in moving patients through the system from prisons, special hospitals, RSUs, NHS hospitals and finally out into community facilities, that services are over-burdened and that appropriate placements for offender patients, especially those presenting long-term behavioural problems, are often difficult to find.

9.2 Diversion from the Criminal Justice System

Considerations of justice as well as of expediency point to the desirability of preventing mentally disordered individuals being unnecessarily caught up in the criminal justice system. The Commission welcomes the support given to efforts at diversion in the Home Office circular (66/90), which draws attention to Sections 136, 38, 35, 36 of the 1983 Act and to the availability of probation orders with treatment requirements. Reasons why these provisions are not being used to the full will be mentioned later.

Ease of access by courts to community and hospital mental health services greatly influences the likelihood of appropriate decisions on diversion being made and implemented. The Home Office circular describes some experimental liaison schemes whereby courts are provided with a duty psychiatrist, for example in Peterborough and at Bow Street, London. A scheme operating in Hetfordshire makes use of multi-disciplinary assessment panels convened ad hoc according to the likely requirements of individual offenders. Liaison schemes work more easily where bail information schemes are also in operation so that probation officers can interview accused persons in custody and pass on background information of use in bail and disposal decisions. Experience suggests that liaison schemes are beneficial and result in markedly increased rates of discontinuance and of hospital admissions. They improve information on the access to existing sevices. They are, however, dependent on the enthusiasm of individuals. They lack systematic organisational and financial support from central authority, they are sometimes hampered by poor facilities, for instance in arrangements for psychiatric examinations, communications between services and the transportation of patients. Unless these schemes can be properly constituted and formally recognised and funded by the appropriate authority the arrangements are likely to prove temporary.

Many offenders with treatment needs for serious mental health problems are committed to prison because they are unsuited to presently available community placements but are not considered detainable under the Mental Health Act. They include many substance abusers, alcoholics, sex offenders and individuals with gross personality disorders. Given appropriate specialised facilities some of these people could be dealt with by means of a probation order with a requirement to undergo treatment. In some cases, however, their behaviour is so persistently disturbed or episodically aggressive that they could be legitimately dealt with under the Act as "psychopaths", but this is rarely done because the staff of NHS hospitals have become very reluctant to accept patients with such a label, considering them unmanageable and untreatable. With less dismissive attitudes and the setting up of specialised units, more of these challenging problems could be taken on board. Prisons would be relieved of some unsuitably placed inmates and the public interest better served by a more constructive approach, but as with many proposals for improvement more resources would need to be channelled into services for this group of individuals.

9.3 Mentally Disturbed Persons in Public (Section 136)

The use of section 136 has been recommended as a means of avoiding unnecessary court appearances of mentally disordered people but the frequency of usage of this section for this purpose and the procedures involved vary greatly from one area to another. This approach needs to be monitored carefully. The enormous differences in practice reflect not only local attitudes but also the difficulty the psychiatric services experience in some districts in making an adequate response. The issue of adherence to desirable practices, mentioned in previous Biennial Reports, remains a concern. Visiting Commissioners are still hearing of instances of persons being taken to a police station for a second officer to decide whether or not it is a case of Section 136. This points to the need in some areas for a continuing educational programme for police officers so that those likely to be involved in making a decision during encounters in a public place are familiar with the requirements of the Act.

The Commission has taken the view, in conformity with that of the Home Office, that a location within a hospital complex is usually preferable to a police station as a place of safety. It is recognised that in many rural areas it may not be practical for hospitals always to be used, and that in some places hospital-based crisis teams find it convenient to visit police stations. Nevertheless, the unquiet atmosphere of some stations, being surrounded by uniformed police and being locked in a police cell can sometimes exacerbate disturbance. The Commission continues to receive reports of police surgeons being called to decide whether a patient should be sent to hospital for a Section 136 assesment. If an assessment is to begin, an ASW should be called without delay. If taken to a police station as a place of safety the person should not be transported elsewhere for Section 136 assessment.

The Commission believes that satisfactory arrangements for Section 136 assessments require the joint preparation of detailed policies by Health Authorities, Local Authority Social Services and the Police. Visiting teams have been pleased to be told of ongoing consultations between authorities. Sometimes, however, it is discovered at subsequent visits that agreed policies are not being implemented, having lapsed through difficulties encountered or through the senior police officer involved having been transferred. It is urged that Section 136 policies, once in place, should be monitored, the dialogue between services continued and arrangements updated when necessary. Good procedures have been developed in London Metropolitan Police areas, in Devon and Cornwall and elsewhere, but a satisfactory policy agreed by all concerned is still to be worked out in some places.

9.4 Difficulties in the Admission of Forensic Cases

The Mental Health Act, in Sections 35 and 36, provides for remands to hospital for psychiatric examination, the intention being to avoid exposing mentally disordered persons to the rigours of a remand to prison. These provisions are still being used very sparingly and unevenly between different hospitals. In 1988/9, there were only 328 remands under Section 35 compared to 5,569 psychiatric reports carried out by prison medical officers following a remand in custody. One reason for this, cited in the Second Biennial Report (p.47), is that consent to treatment provisions do not apply to Section 35 remands, although the Commission takes the view that in certain rare instances, the use of a concurrent Section 3 may be appropriate. Psychiatric hospital staff are also concerned about security and suitability of the physical environment for these patients. Section 36 is even less used, but this is because of there being numerically fewer cases from the Crown Court.

Psychiatric opinions as to the usefulness of Section 35 vary. Some have suggested that preparation of medical reports pretrial would permit immediate operation of a hospital order (Section 37) or at least an interim order (Section 38). The Commission has also heard the opinion that admission under Section 35 is inappropriate until the individual has been examined in prison, a view which appears to negate the purpose of the provision. The Commssion hopes that in due course the psychiatric remand provisions of the Mental Heath Act will be reviewed with the aim of making them more useful.

The Commission is aware that large numbers of minor offenders with known mental health problems enter the penal system. Although they have the legal power to do so, magistrates' practice of remanding to prison solely for the purpose of obtaining reports is regrettable. It often reflects the problem of finding a place for the many offenders without accommodation or finding an appropriate venue for out-patient examination. The fact that remand to prison is the most convenient option is not without influence. In many instances where it would seem relevant magistrates fail to obtain a psychiatric opinion and recommendation, often because they doubt it would prove helpful since consultant psychiatrists at district level feel unable to help the courts. The court psychiatry liaison schemes cited earlier have had a favourable impact only in the limited areas in which they operate.

The inability of district psychiatric services to respond promptly to the needs of the courts stems from a number of causes. The demands are not seen as part of the mainstream service and are not therefore planned for. Secure beds are often lacking. Rapid management and structural changes have also reduced capacity to respond. Places for difficult patients needing long term care are not available and there are also conflicts between professional staff about the appropriateness of institutional or community care for individual patients.

Those coming before the courts accused of more serious crimes are dealt with by the crown Courts and have the advantage that opinion and assessment will normally be sought from the regional forensic psychiatric service and/or the special hospitals. All Regions in England and Wales now have forensic psychiatrists in post to assist in these cases.

Use is made of interim hospital orders under Section 38 and 39 which provide ample time for evaluation in hospital and the compilation of medical recommendations for the courts. Referrals to the forensic service come from the courts, the defendant's solicitor, the Crown Prosecution Service or the Prison Medical Service. Most of these cases have been initially remanded in custody.

How soon referrals and admissions take place appears rather haphazard. Transfer for assessment and treatment may occur within a week or be delayed many months. One reason for this wide variation is the limited availability of secure beds in RSUs. Provision of services in secure units is considered below.

9.5 Restricted Patients

Offender patients judged by the courts to be a general danger to the public and therefore detained under restriction orders under section 41 present particular difficulties. The order is imposed by the trial judge in the light of medical evidence and recommendations and carries the power of conditional discharge. Many such patients are accepted in the first instance by the Special Hospitals, although a small number go to RSUs and to local district hospitals. Most of those admitted to Special Hospitals are expected to be transferred to regional or district facilities before their ultimate release into the community, but delays in transfer (described in greater detail elsewhere in this report) are often unacceptably long. With the reduction in secure facilities in psychiatric units and the creation of small district units, sometimes of twenty or fewer beds the Commission has found areas where district psychiatrists feel quite unable to cope with restricted patients, either in the first instance or at the stage of rehabilitation. There is now a tendency to perceive restricted patients and forensic psychiatry in general as a specialist concern so that the needs of these patients become marginalised and the necessary nursing skills are lost. A lack of confidence between the Home Office and the supervising RMO in the local psychiatric hospital can also lead to delays and difficulties in obtaining permission for parole and rehabilitation activities. These problems result in unfair discrimination against restricted patients.

9.6 Difficulties in the Discharge of Offender Patients

Mentally disordered offenders who are not restricted can be discharged from their detaining section either by their RMO or by order of a Review Tribunal. Restricted patients may be conditionally or absolutely discharged by a Tribunal or by the Home Secretary. Before discharge, however, there must be agreement on a plan for some degree of follow up, supervision and social re-integration. Authorities are reminded that mentally disordered offenders are covered by Section 117, which places a responsibility jointly on health authorities and social services authorities to arrange joint aftercare arrangements.

The discharge or transfer of patients from Special Hospitals involves negotiating the obstacle of ownership of responsibility for the patient, that is, determining which district, which hospital, which local authoirty which doctor or which RSU should make provision. Requests for places are often refused on grounds of inability of a local authority to obtain funding or unwillingness of the consultant concerned to recognise the patient as belonging to his or her catchment area. Patients of no fixed abode may be disowned by the area of choice if some distant relative or history of prior hospitalisation can be discovered elsewhere. These unseemly squabbles can lead to protracted delays and RHAs are asked to ensure they have an effective mechanism for handling promptly any problems arising in their District.

Discharges from RSUs depend on a range of outlets to which patients may be moved. For those on Restriction Orders there is first the issue of obtaining Home Office permission, which may take months and sometimes over a year. A constant complaint made to the Commission is that it is impossible to obtain a suitable placement when no firm date can be given while a Home Office decision is still pending. Obversely, the Home Office may refuse to agree to discharge until clear plans are available. This "Catch 22" situation produces pressure to agree to whatever the Home Office proposes regardless of the patient's true needs. Long waits cause staff frustration, collapse of rehabilitation programmes and great distress to patients.

When RSUs are ready to discharge they are dependent on other district NHS facilities, purpose built accommodation and social services. Each Unit has access to a different level of provision. Some (e.g. Mersey) have developed their own cluster of homes. Some units rely on landladies and neighbouring hospitals, but many district rehabilitation services reject offender patients as too difficult. Some forensic services (e.g. West Midlands) have built up their own after care service. Others are obliged by geography or limited resources to rely on local districts.

The provision of social work services to offender patients remains haphazard. Some local authorities provide only minimum statutory cover for Review Tribunals and discharge planning. Some who provided social work input to RSUs have reduced staff levels as a result of financial pressures. Many local authorities regard such patients as too few in number and too specialised to warrant time and attention. There are concerns that very little of the specific grant money allocated in 1990 has been earmarked for this group of patients. Posts for liaison with Special Hospitals and for planning for the needs of their patients, such as were set up by Avon county council, have disappeared.

The statutory supervisors of offender patients on Home Office licence within the community have an individual and onerous responsibility and the Home Office has issued formal advice. The changing nature of psychiatric care and the trend towards generic mental health social work services means that many senior officers are not now conversant with this type of work. The Commission welcomes guidelines for supervisors of restricted patients which have been introduced by Wiltshire County Council and other local authorities. The Home Office and Regional forensic services have participated helpfully in training days and joint seminars in some areas.

Non-restricted mentally disordered offenders also require careful after care to ensure their stability within the community. The reality today is that in some areas, especially in inner London, these patients are sometimes discharged to bed and breakfast accommodation with no more care than a vague arrangement for out-patient appointment (to be notified by letter later) or for a visit from a community psychiatric nurse. In some boroughs bed and breakfast provision is arranged in a locality outside the psychiatric catchment area. Although on paper there may appear to be a good care plan as required by Section 117, in reality its effectiveness depends on the co-operation of the patient and the constant commitment of a small number of dedicated professionals. Such tenuous arrangements frequently break down; the patients' mental health may deteriorate and they frequently

reappear in the criminal justice system, or another psychiatric service. The practice of discharging detained patients to unsatisfactory temporary accommodation is to be deplored and is totally unacceptable for mentally disordered offenders. It reflects a serious lack in mental health services of management action to prevent it. A joint approach by health and social services is essential to ensure that the Care Programme approach is properly implemented for patients discharged from Section 37.

9.7 Granting Leave of Absence (Section 17)

Section 17, whereby a RMO may grant leave of absence from hospital with the imposition of any conditions considered necessary, is a helpful device in a patient's rehabilitation programme as a trial of ability to manage successfully outside hospital or in a place of reduced security. Such an arrangement is generally encouraging to the patient whose involvement in its planning is recommended by the Code of Practice. Whilst on leave the patient remains liable to be detained and subject to the provisions for treatment under Part IV of the Act. Occasionally, such leave is properly granted on compassionate grounds or to permit treatment of intercurrent physical disorders.

Other uses of Section 17 to overcome difficulties in management or placement are more questionable. For example, the powers of Section 17 have been employed for the long-term administration of compulsory treatment outside hospital through extended leave and routine recall shortly before its expiry, to permit renewal of a Section 3 and then a return to leave of absence. This practice can no longer be supported following the judgement in the case R v Hallstrom.

In other cases Section 17 has been used to move a patient presenting severe management problems from a district hospital to an RSU. A limited period of intensive care at the RSU is then followed by return to the district hospital where the patient has remained liable to be detained. It is the Commission's view that such a procedure is contrary to the intentions of Section 17. Inevitably the move takes place during an acute phase of mental disorder and removes the patient from easy access to his RMO and managers under the Act at the district hospital, who have specific powers regarding consent to treatment and discharge. At such a time, a patient cannot be involved in the decision for leave, as recommended by the Code of Practice. The root cause of the use of Section 17 in this way lies in the reluctance of some district hospitals to accept the return of particularly difficult patients once transferred out of their care and the inability of RSUs to offer long-term care. In the long run, the establishment of long-term care facilities for difficult-to-manage patients is required for every District. Meanwhile, a standard transfer of full care to the RSU for limited time is preferable to use of Section 17 leave which gives the patient both necessary treatment and maximum protection of rights under the Act.

Leave of absence from hospital under section 17 is often a major component of rehabilitation programmes. Such leave may cover periods of absence from a single night up to six months. Short term absences of only a few hours also feature extensively in treatment plans and are sometimes regarded as a form of parole arranged at ward level in the hospital. The Act, however, describes leave of absence without mention of its duration whilst its granting is the prerogative solely of the RMO. The occurrence of any untoward incidents during absence from hospital could raise the question of its planning and authorization. On the other hand the requirement to obtain RMO agreement for every activity outside the hospital would seriously curtail any patient's involvement in the social programme and other rehabilitative activities which are often arranged at short notice by ward staff. The recommendation of the Commission is that all absences from hospital should be regarded as constituting leave with a need for RMO authorization but that such leave should be agreed periodically, the weekly multidisciplinary conference being an ideal occasion, with a written statement of the maximum licence that is granted for a defined period and with any related conditions. Staff implementing the treatment programme would then be free to arrange absences from hospital within the known limits and without need to obtain further more detailed authorizations.

The Commission has recently been investigating a complaint from a former unrestricted patient at Broadmoor which involves the interpretation of an RMO's point to grant leave of absence in relation to the hospital authorization: duty to ensure the safety of the patient and the public. The Commission will be issuing its report towards the end of 1991.

9.8 Difficult to Place Patients

Patients who are difficult to place do not necessarily come via the courts. What characterises them is that all parts of the psychiatric service, have a different reason for not wanting them. Consequently they tend, when not shuttling between all the district, regional and Special Hospitals, to be dealt with by prison, general practitioners and private hospitals. The Special Hospitals deem them not dangerous to the public at large. The RSUs see them as needing some degree of containment only intermittently and regard them as properly the responsibility of local services. District psychiatric services feel unable to devote a relatively large proportion of their limited capital and revenue resources to providing the special care needed by a very small number of individuals. Most such patients are known by name to all concerned. When Commissioners visit health authorities they are typically told of two or three such cases. Some districts have plans for dealing with this small group, others have had such plans but have now shelved them due to regional cut backs on capital or revenue shortfalls. Bath Health Authority, for example, is unable to use their recently constructed, purpose built six-bedded unit for lack of revenue. By default, many of these difficult to manage patients are in private care. The allocation of long term, difficult and unwanted patients to the private sector means that local knowledge and expertise in the NHS is being lost. Placement decisions are often taken by unit managers and clinicians on behalf of Health Authorities without them realising what is being done in their name. Some RSUs are pressured to take in such patients but this inevitably impairs the units' ability to respond to the demands of the courts. Some districts have recognised that a comprehensive service should have provision for this small group of difficult patients. They include some short term acutely ill as well as those with long term needs. Districts need to collaborate on establishing units which serve perhaps several adjoining districts, which are geographically well located but able to meet the diverse needs of both short and long term patients.

9.9 Funding

The restructuring of the NHS in 1991/2 has introduced further complications of funding into the various arrangements. These affect particularly offender patients and especially those with long term needs. The Commission has seen protracted correspondence, lasting months or years, between managers, doctors and social workers attempting to establish who should be paying the revenue costs of such patients. In one region patients coming before the courts are being committed to private care, the bill for which subsequently arrives at the door of the District Health Authority where it has to be met by a psychiatric service that has had no say in the proceedings. This practice should of course encourage local Districts to plan ahead for this group of patients but has an unreasonable impact on current services. Despite meetings between forensic psychiatrists and the Department of Health to try to clarify the funding and revenue issues for regional services, the system remains unclear and differing operational arrangements exist at local and national level across the country. The Commission's concern is for offender patients whose access to services depends on explicit rules for funding. At present patients and their advocates are frequently left in the dark as to which authority should accept financial responsibility for providing care.

9.10 Legal Assistance for Offender Patients

Offender patients are often dependent on the advocacy role of the legal profession for obtaining access to service. The present problems with Legal Aid have meant that fewer and fewer firms are taking on criminal work and fewer solicitors and barristers are ready to become involved in the difficult area of mental health. The Commission sees a pressing need for the Law Society to promote the development of a system in which every major centre of population has an accessible body of professionals who fully understand the workings of mental health law. This would contribute to the development of a comprehensive psychiatric service covering the admissions, transfers and discharges of detained mentally disordered offenders.

9.11 Secure Units other than Special Hospitals

Progress in the provision of RSUs was reported in the 1987–89 Biennial Report. A review of the position in the summer of 1991 reveals underachievement in meeting well recognised and urgent needs:

(a) The need

The Butler Committee regarded the provision of secure hospital units in *each* RHA area as such a priority that it presented an interim report in July 1974 (Cmnd 5698) calling for that provision "as a matter of urgency".

Features of the envisaged units included—
  i. High staff to patient ratios.
  ii. Educational facilities.
  iii. Permanent social work staff.
  iv. Regional siting reasonably near to the patient's home and family both for relieving the psychiatric hospitals and special hospitals and for receiving patients from prisons and the courts.

The DHSS reacted by calling upon RHA to take action for the early establishment of RSUs. Initially the aim was to provide 1000 places (on a roughly 20 per million of population basis) to be followed by an increase to the figure of 2000 recommended by the Butler Committee if the need was confirmed by experience, and when resources permitted. The Department would make direct supplementary financial allocations to Regions to facilitate establishment of the units.

Implementation of the policy was both slow and patchy. In May 1991 the Department of Health recorded that there were 21 RSUs established in 13 RHA areas and a 14th area was about to have its first unit approved. There are still only some 600 beds in RSUs and a small number of interim secure unit beds. Thus 17 years after 1000 places were said to be needed as a matter of urgency, 330–400 places remain unprovided.

The shortfall of places has been met by rapid expansion of places in independent sector mental nursing homes. There are now approximately 1100 places in private hospitals. While this private provision has provided suitable placement and valuable care for some difficult and offender patients, it has not provided a completely satisfactory substitute for a locally based service near to patients homes.

(b) Current regional services

The high ratio of nursing staff to patients has generally been achieved. These units have become valuable centres of skill and experience in dealing with particularly violent and disruptive patients providing advice and training for other psychiatric hospitals in the region.

The following regions still fall short of the basic provision of 20 beds per million of the population: North East Thames, Northern, North West Thames, Oxford, South West Thames, Trent, Wessex, West Midlands, York and Wales, of which the poorest provision for their populations is North East Thames, South West Thames and Wales. While the Commision recognises that these two regions and Wales have definite plans to provide an increased local service, it must be said that for some years they have been long on plans and short on action. The use of private sector facilities in Hertfordshire has been particularly notable in North East Thames for patients from City and Hackeny, Tower Hamlets and Newham Health Authorities are at an inconvenient distance from patients homes and the use of a distant RSU for Welsh patients. All regions are asked to review their current provision against knowledge of local need.

The consequences of the current shortfall are transfer delays from Special Hospitals, delayed transfer for mentally ill prisoners, the management of very difficult patients in general psychiatric units poorly designed for their needs and sometimes leading to the use of heavy sedative medication, and the loss of valuable opportunities to advance the educational development of patients. An example of the long delays experienced was brought to the attention of visiting Commissioners at Ravenswood Forensic Unit, Knowle Hospital in June 1991. A disturbed young man charged with burglaries had been kept in prison on remand for a year while attempts were made to transfer him under Section 48. Various RSUs had been unable to offer him a place until he was finally admitted to Ravenswood.

9.12 Education in RSUs

In chapter 13 of its Third Biennial Report the Commission raised issues about special provisions of patients by Local Education Authorities (LEA) for the educational needs of patients suffering from mental disorder. It was indicated that the Commission would be pursuing these matters and it has done so with both the Department of Health (DH) and the Department of Education and Science (DES). The Commission was represented at a conference on educational provision in NHS secure units in February 1991 at which suggestions emerged which the Commission would support. At present RSUs in which education is provided

finance it in various ways. It is recommended that a common funding policy for education should be established. The DES should set standards of quality for this service. LEAs should provide a senior educational manager in the planning stage and a support group to back up the work.

9.13 The Mentally Disordered in Prison

In August, 1990, the Commission submitted evidence to the Woolf Inquiry arguing that the Commission's remit sould be extended to protect the rights and interests of mentally disordered prisoners in prison hospitals. While the Commission would urge that immediate steps be taken to prevent mentally disordered people from joining the prison population, whether as remand or as sentenced prisoners, it recognises that a number of mentally disordered people will inevitably remain in prison. These people will continue to require special consideration and are entitled to expect an adequate standard of medical and nursing care While in prison they have no choice but to rely exclusively on that which is provided for them within the penal establishment.

The Commission has noted that the Social Services Committee (SSC) received much evidence of mentally disordered prisoners held in appalling conditions (Minutes of Evidence taken before SSC, Session 1985–6, and the Third Report from the SSC, Prison Medical Service, HMSO 1986). The report of HM Chief Inspector into Prison Suicides (HMSO Cm 1383, Dec 1990) serves only to confirm that progress has been slow.

In 1989 the High Court heard evidence of the conditions in the hospital wing at Brixton Prison where a mentally disordered prisoner had hanged himself while awaiting a bed in an NHS facility. The High Court held that the law did not impose the same standard of care on the prison authorities as would be applied to an NHS unit, but refused "to speculate on what an appropriate standard might be" (Knight v The Home Office 1 December 1989, unreported). The Commission feels that the absence of guidance is unfortunate and believes that the need to improve the conditions for mentally disordered prisoners is urgent. Forty eight prisoners died at their own hands in 1989 and a further forty two in the first ten months of 1990.

Mentally disordered people in prison are often receiving medical care of some kind but outside the structure of the NHS and are therefore denied the benefit of the usual NHS complaints mechanisms. The Commssion advocates that, in penal establishments which possess clearly defined hospital wings, these areas should be designated as hospitals and brought under NHS supervision. The Commission would then urge that it be given jurisdiction to enter such "hospitals" and "keep under review the care and treatment" of mentally disordered people accommodated therein. Such prisoner/patients would not be detained under the Mental Health Act but the Commission believes that, since they would be both mentally disordered and detained in the ordinary sense of the term, they would resemble its present client group in these two essential respects. The Commission could both monitor an agreed Code of practice and act as an independent channel for complaints. Unlike HM Chief Inspector of Prisons (Suicide Report, supra) however, the Commssion would not envisage the application of the consent provisions within Part IV of the Act to these prison hospitals. Indeed it would urge that, while prison hospitals should be designated hospitals and run by NHS personnel, they should be disqualified from accommodating patients detained under the Mental Health Act. If a prisoner is sufficiently disordered or requires compulsory treatment in hospital, he or she should be transferred to a psychiatric unit in the ordinary way, whether it's to be a local facility or to a Special Hospital.

These considerations have implications for the plan (set out in a preliminary way in the *Report on an Efficiency Scrutiny of the Prison Medical Service*, July 1990) to transform the role of the service from a provider of health care to that of a purchaser. Clinicians from "the wider health community" would work under contract in the prisons, either on a part time or on a short term secondment basis. While this might help to bring standards into line with those of the NHS, the Commission is concerned that, so long as some categories of mentally disordered offenders have to be kept in prison, there should be a stable clinical staff responsible for continuity of care and for arranging transfers whenever possible.

After the publication of the Report of the Woolf Inquiry in February, 1991, the Chairman of the Commission wrote to the Home Secretary repeating the views expressed in the Commission's evidence to the Inquiry and suggesting, as a minimum alternative to an extension of the Commission's remit, the involvement of the Commission on the newly constituted boards of visitors. This would be a means of monitoring prisoners who receive treatment for mental disorder outside of hospital wings.

9.14 Section 47/49

The Commission believes that it is essential that the prison service is in a position both to provide speedy assessment of mental disorder and to achieve the smooth transfer to hospital of those fulfilling the criteria of the Act. It has been noted however that mentally disordered prisoners are often transferred towards the end of prisoners' sentences. The Commission is aware of a number of worrying cases where transfers took place very close to the prisoner's release date. The Commission believes that such late transfers are unacceptable save insofar as newly emerging disorders are concerned, and thus places considerable emphasis on the need to ensure swift and accurate assessment within prison. The Commission is pleased to find this view endorsed by the Interdepartmental Working Group on Mentally Disturbed Offenders in the Prison System (Report paras 2(vi) and 6.20) and it also welcomes the reference to early transfers in the Code of Practice (Para 3.4) and the emphasis on early assessment and speedy transfer in the Home Office Circular 66/90 (paras 23 and 24).

While swift assessment is essential to the smooth transfer to hospital of the mentally disordered, such transfer cannot occur in the absence of adequate facilities outside prison. However, the Commission believes that an integration of the prison psychiatric services with local NHS provision would greatly facilitate the transfer of offenders from prison to hospital. This is perhaps particularly true of those prisoners who do not require the security of a Special Hospital or RSU. The early involvement of local NHS consultants, who need not be forensic specialists, might ease some of the problems of transfer.

The question of return to prison at the conclusion of their treatment in hospital of prisoners transferred to hospital under Section 47/49 has recently been considered by the Commssion. In cases where the patient has been in custody for a period to serve in prison, and where the patient's RMO or the Tribunal indicates to the Home Secretary that the patient no longer requires treatment in hospital for mental disorder, the Commssion would like to see the introduction

of a presumption that the patient would be discharged from hospital into the community by way of the Act. The Home Secretary could of course rebut the presumption in any particular case where he thought a return to prison was desirable.

9.15 Life Sentence Transfers

The discharge procedures for life sentence transferees has been a source of special concern to the Commission particularly in relation to the identification of the precise "tariff" of years to be detained, the respective roles of the MHRT and the Parole Board, and the delays experienced by some transferees. The Commssion is also aware of the difficulties faced by Special Hospital doctors who are required to treat transferred life sentence prisoners without knowing whether they are to be prepared for discharge via the hospital system or for eventual return to prison.

Following the decision of the European Court of Human Rights in *Thynne, Wilson and Gunnell v The United Kingdom*, the government is amending the procedures for the release of discretionary life sentence prisoners. At present the Commission is still uncertain precisely what form these new procedures will take, but it has urged the government to take the opportunity offered by the need to comply with the European Convention to rationalise the system for the release of all transferred lifers.

In particular the Commission would welcome any moves to open up and formalise the setting of the tariff period in individual cases. The Commission believes that the uncertainty which can surround the tariff date is unfortunate for both the transferees and for those attempting to provide an appropriate treatment programme preparing them for discharge. Further the Commission understands that a specially empowered PD will be made responsible for the release of discretionary lifers, and would urge that thought be given to the relationship between this board and the MHRT in the case of lifers transferred to hospital. It would seem unnecessary and time-consuming to subject a transferred lifer, whose tariff has expired while he is in hospital, to scrutiny by two separate tribunals prior to release. The Commission would like the govenment to explore the possibility of enabling (through legislative amendment if necessary) a special hybrid tribunal to hear the cases of transferred lifers in hospital. This would enable the prisoner patient's mental state, his or her suitability for compulsory treatment and likely dangerousness to be assessed at one time, while he or she is still in hospital, by the body empowered to authorise discharge. The Commission has also urged the government, whatever its attitude to mandatory lifers within the prison system, to apply the same procedures to all lifers transferred to hospital, whether their life sentence be mandatory or discretionary. The Commission feels that to differentiate between the two types of sentence once the patient is in hospital would be quite unjustified, and likely to lead to confusion on the part of hospital staff and to an understandable sense of injustice on the part of the transferees.

10.
SERVICES FOR PEOPLE WITH LEARNING DIFFICULTIES

10.1 Introduction

The Commission has established a People With Learning Disabilities National Standing Committee which keeps under review issues relating to mentally impaired and severely mentally impaired detained patients.

10.2 Lack of Specialised Services

The Commission is very concerned about the patchy and inadequate development of services for people with learning disabilities who are mentally ill, who have behaviour problems or who offend. The need for specialised facilities is becoming increasingly acute as the mental handicap hospital closure programme gathers pace. Although there are well established and excellent services in some Health Districts, in many there is a paucity of facilities for assessment, treatment and aftercare and a worrying lack of firm plans for future provision. Patients with special needs from these Districts often end up in inappropriate placements or in placements many miles away from their homes and families. The Commission recently visited the secure unit at Borocourt Hospital, West Berkshire Health Authority. This unit provides 14 beds and on visiting the unit Commissioners noted that many patients in this unit had a diagnosis of mental impairment. The future of this unit is uncertain and the hospital closure is planned to take place by 1993.

The Commission is particularly worried by the lack of appropriate facilities for learning disabled people who offend. Specialised Medium Secure Units for this group of patients are available in only four NHS Regions at the moment and semi-secure provision is equally sparse. In consequence, many learning disabled offenders are inappropriately admitted to Regional Secure Units for mentally ill people, or placed in private or other facilities far from home, often remanded in custody for long periods awaiting placement or even worse, may receive a prison sentence. Lack of specialised provision also has a significant impact in delaying transfers from the Special Hospitals. The number of mentally impaired and severely mentally impaired people on the transfer list at Rampton Hospital has risen from 21 in 1987 to 35 in 1991. At Ashworth Hospital there are 18 mentally handicapped people on the transfer delay list, several of whom have experienced very significant delay.

Many of the local hospitals that in the past accepted patients have stopped admitting as they get closer to their final closing down date. For example in one case a woman patient has been on the transfer list at Rampton Hospital since 1988. A unit in the local hospital would have been appropriate but is now closed to admissions, so she must wait until a housing project being set up by Rampton can get past the planning stage.

A number of patients are awaiting new facilities which in some cases have yet to be built. An example is that of a woman patient who has been considered for transfer since 1989, but as she has a tendency to wander off she must remain at Rampton Hospital until such time as she has progressed sufficiently to reside on an open ward or to wait for the building of a Medium Secure Unit that is still in the planning stage.

New private facilities are developing to provide for some of the needs but the funding of such placements is now a growing problem. In another case known to the Commission a Special Hospital patient who could not be offered a place in a local hospital near her home was offered a placement in a private institution. The Finance Director of the local Health Authority subsequently confirmed that they were unable to fund the placement. The patient is still on the waiting list for a local hospital.

10.3 Rehabilitation and Aftercare Services

Specialised rehabilitation and aftercare services are required for these patients who do not generally fit satisfactorily in regular community facilities for mentally handicapped people because they require a different therapeutic approach and more structure and supervision. Lack of such facilities is a frequent cause of breakdown and reinstitutionalisation.

10.4 Conclusion

Two reports, one from a Department of Health study team "Needs and Responses: Services for adults with mental handicap who are mentally ill, who have behaviour problems or who offend" (1989) and one from the Welsh Office "Challenges and Responses" (May, 1991) have been published. Both provide excellent accounts of the needs and service requirements of these groups of patients and are commended to all Health Authorities and Social Services Departments.

11.
LEGAL MATTERS

11.1 The Witham case

Throughout the period covered by both the 3rd and 4th Biennial reports the Commission has been engaged in two separate law suits brought at the instance of Mr Mark Witham, an informal patient for whom a consultant psychiatrist had prescribed a drug to dampen Mr Witham's sexual drive. The drug, Goserelin (trade name Zoladex) had been licensed for treatment of carcinoma of the testes. It had not hitherto been used for treating sexually deviant patients. The drug was administered by means of long-acting depot injections.

In August 1987 an application was made to the Commission to make appointment under Section 57 of the Mental Health Act, by virtue of Regulation 16(1) of the Mental Health Regulations 1983 which provides for certification procedure of Section 57 for any "surgical implantation of hormones for the purpose of reducing male sex drive" when this treatment is for mental disorder. In the event the drug, Goserelin, was held by the High Court not to be hormone, but in fact an anti-hormone, and the mode of injection did not involve "surgical implantation". Hence there was no requirement on the part of the patient's doctor to seek a certificate under Section 57, and the Commission had no jurisdiction to make any appointments.

The patient applied for judicial review challenging the decisions of the three persons appointed by the Commission not to give a certificate on the grounds that the patient did not fully understand the nature and likely effects of the drug and that the medication prescribed was not an appropriate treatment for the condition. The High Court in May 1988 upheld jurisdiction and questioned the decision of the three appointees. Had the court not decided that the appointments under Section 57 were null and void it would still have questioned the decision of the three appointees on the grounds they performed their task. Since then the Commission has separated the medical function of deciding the appropriateness of the treatment from the duty of the appointees to satisfy themselves that the patient's consent to treatment is informed and real.

The patient brought a civil action in January 1991 alleging negligence against the three appointees in a number of respects and went on to claim that the Commission was ultimately responsible in law for such negligence.

On 12 July Mr Witham's claim was struck out on the main ground that the duties under Section 57 (and Section 58) were performable exclusively within the field of public law, for breaches of which judicial review was the sole remedy. No liability in private law could arise.

Mr Witham was granted leave to appeal but the Court of Appeal is unlikely to hear the case until the end of 1991.

The Commission has welcomed the opportunity this case has provided to focus on its procedures for operating both Section 57 and Section 58 of the Act. A new procedure has been established for Section 57, described more fully in Chapter 6 (Consent to Treatment) of this report. Furthermore, the Commission now appoints to the panel of persons who operate Section 57 procedures registered medical practitioners and other persons who are not current members of the Mental Health Act Commission in addition to current Commission members.

11.2 The Law Commission Consultation Paper No 119 — Mentally Incapacitated Adults and Decision-Making

The MHAC welcomes this valuable discussion document which sets out a number of options for amending the decision making law on care and treatment of mentally incapacitated adults. The Commission has drawn attention in previous biennial reports to the many difficulties which relatives and professionals experience in making appropriate decisions for these individuals, who may be living in their family homes, or in residential care or in hospital wards; many are de facto detained in order to provide care and protection. At present there is an absence of any legal provision for most of the decisions made on behalf of mentally incapacitated adults.

The issues addressed by the Mental Health Act Commission in our response to the Law Commission included: the need for reform; the principles and values which should apply to decision making on behalf of mentally incapacitated people; principles in guiding the application of tests of incapacity; and the decision making processes on behalf of mentally incapacitated adults.

(a) The need for reform

The Commission recognises that changes in the law are time consuming and disruptive and should not be contemplated unless absolutely necessary, but the case for reform in this area is apparent. At present, the absence of suitable procedures for social, financial and educational as well as medical decisions on behalf of people unable to act for themselves, causes difficulties for the individuals themselves, their families and professionals. In particular, disputes between professionals or within families can lead to action or inaction which is clearly contrary to the best interests of the person concerned.

(b) Principles and values

Three principles appropriate to decision making on behalf of mentally incapacitated adults are probably now widely accepted.

i. **autonomy:** the individual must be given the freedom to determine his or her own life to the greatest possible extent, provided she/he does not infringe the freedom of others.

ii. **normalisation:** the availability of adequate resources and positive social attitudes are the two essential features of a successful policy based upon a principle of normalisation.

iii. **provision of safeguards without stigma:** where decisions need to be taken on behalf of an incapacitated person, this should not set the individual apart from his or her fellows.

Two further principles are likely to give rise to debate but are nevertheless recommended by the Commission.

iv. **the presumption of capacity:** Traditionally in health matters it is only when the patient disagrees with a proposed course of treatment that the question of capacity arises. If the patient does not express disagreement then capacity is deemed to exist. It is important at certain critical events that an individual's capacity and therefore autonomy to make decisions is determined.

v. **the best interests standard:** The Commission recommends the application of the 'best interests standard' in preference to the principle of 'substituted judgement'. The only exception to this recommendation is when the decision maker *knows* of the wishes/views or beliefs expressed when the person was capable, for example through a binding Living Will.

(c) Tests of incapacity

The Commission proposes two quite separate procedures: one to decide whether an individual is incapacitated and a second to organise the decision making where incapacity is found. The Commission recommends that capacity be determined by an appropriately qualified *independent* person (someone other than the person responsible for care or a course of treatment).

(d) Proposals for a panel of protection

The present position is that parents and other carers of mentally incapacitated adults make decisions on their behalf. For certain types of decision professional or expert advice is sought from doctors, social workers, nurses, residential care staff, lawyers and others. A limited number of people have their affairs managed by the Court of Protection and many more by appointees.

In the vast majority of situations this predominantly informal decision making works well. Nevertheless the Commission concluded that a new structure is needed for the following reasons.

i. to clarify the legal basis of decisions currently taken by parents, relatives, carers and others.

ii. to allow a procedure to resolve cases where there is a dispute between parents, carers, relatives and others or within families.

iii. to resolve cases where the incapacitated person is thought to be at risk of neglect, injury or an inappropriate life style.

iv. to facilitate decision making where this would be in the best interests of the incapacitated person.

The Commission supports the view that every Social Services area should have a Panel of Protection to provide the legal framework for difficult or controversial decision making on behalf of mentally incapacitated adults. A three level administrative structure is proposed to enable the appointment and monitoring of decision makers.

At the first level the Panel would formally appoint decision makers; review those appointments at specified intervals; oversee the registration of decision makers; review the decision making procedures within residential establishments; ensure that registration is based upon the proper application of approved tests of capacity; and issue guidelines for tests of capacity and the decision making process for mentally incapacitated adults.

The second level would involve decisions by a single Panel member of 'primary reviewer'. This resource could be called upon in the event of a dispute between a family member and a professional, for example. Other second level decisions would involve specified medical treatments such as elective surgery; personal decisions affecting the residence or overall care arrangements of the individual; and some financial decisions.

Third level decisions would be made by a committee of three or more members of the Panel. Decisions where disagreement had not been resolved by the primary reviewer would be referred to the third level; also the most important decisions affecting the individual's life.

The Commission would like to see a specialised national tribunal which would hear appeals by interested parties against the decisions of district panels in relation to both third level decisions and the registration of decision makers.

('The response to the Law Commission Working Paper on Mentally Incapacitated Adults and Decision Making' is available from the Mental Health Act Commission)

11.3 The Mental Health Act 1983

It is now eight years since the Act came into force and there is considerable experience with its use. The Commission's primary statutory responsibility is to monitor the operation of the 1983 Act.

In the course of such monitoring it has encountered instances which illustrate possible deficiencies in the Act itself. Whilst any future amendment of the Mental Health Act is a matter for Parliament, it may be helpful to draw attention in this report to areas of possible change for consideration by all those with an interest in these matters.

(a) Section 8(1)

The power of Guardianship is disappointingly little used. Many local authorities have expressed concern that the omission of a power to convey a patient to a place of residence or to attend at a place for the purpose of treatment, occupation, education or training seriously undermines the authority of a Guardian and in practice, prevents the Guardianship being used at all in many cases. The Commission would like to suggest that amendments to Sections 8(1)(a) and (b) to allow a power to convey would be very helpful in encouraging the use of this less restrictive form of supervisory order.

(b) Section 12(5)

It would appear to be an anomaly that certain doctors cannot provide the recommendation that a person be detained in certain institutions but they can (and indeed must under Section 20) provide the medical recommendations for the continued detention of the patient beyond the initial period. If the Act is attempting to ensure that there should be no question of financial motives influencing medical recommendations then it is illogical that a doctor with a financial interest should provide the report that allows the detention to continue. It is suggested that Section 12(5) should be amended to ensure consistency by prescribing the renewal of authority to detain a patient under this part of the Act.

(c) Section 12

In many areas there are real difficulties in providing out of hours cover of a rota of Section 12 approved doctors, especially for patients who are already in hospital at the time of the assessment. While the main solution to this problem is for every DHA to ensure that there is a rota of suitably qualified psychiatrists willing to undertake this work, it would also be helpful for there to be suitably trained general practitioners available. It has been suggested that a new subsection could be added to Section 12 to the effect that each FHSA shall keep a rota of general practitioners willing to provide medical recommendations and that each FHSA shall ensure that all such general practitioners are seconded for appropriate training.

(d) Section 29(3)

There have been many instances reported to the Commission where it has been inappropriate for a person to remain as the nearest relative for the purposes of the Act, for instance if the patient has been abused, physically, emotionally or sexually by the nearest relative or, for instance, where the patient and the nearest relative have severed all emotional links. It has been suggested that Section 29(3) could be amended so that an application for an order under this section could be made on any grounds and shall succeed if the following grounds are established:

i. that the patient has no nearest relative within the meaning of the Act, or that it is not reasonably practicable to ascertain whether he has such a relative, or who that relative is;

ii. that the nearest relative of the patient is incapable of acting as such by reason of mental disorder or other illness.

iii. that the nearest relative of the patient unreasonably objects to the making of an application for admission for treatment or a guardianship application in respect of the patient; or,

iv. that the nearest relative of the patient has exercised without due regard to the welfare of the patient or the interest of the public his power to discharge the patient from hospital or guardianship under this Part of this Act, or is likely to do so.

If the application is to succeed upon grounds other than those set out above the Court would have to be satisfied that the application was reasonable and that it was in the best interests of the patient.

(e) Section 35

The infrequent use of Section 35 has been mentioned in Chapter 9, Services for Difficult and Offender Patients. Many psychiatrists have pointed out that it seems to be illogical that a patient detained in hospital sometimes for several months should not be compulsorily treatable. His situation would appear to be the equivalent of a Section 2 patient who is detained for assessment (or assessment followed by medical treatment). The only other patients detained in hospital who cannot be given compulsory treatment are those detained under the very short term sections. It has therefore been suggested that Section 35 needs to be amended to enable RMO's to give treatment without consent where necessary, but that treatment without consent should not be given without a second opinion nor should it be given unless the RMO and the second opinion doctor confirm that the patient, if not detained under Section 35, would be detainable under Sections 2 or 3 of the Mental Health Act 1983. If Section 35 was amended in this way then the reference to Section 35 would need to be deleted in Section 56(1)(b).

(f) Section 73

At present a MHRT can override the clinical opinion of psychiatrists and the opinion of the Home Secretary and order that a restricted patient be allowed his liberty, but only the Home Secretary is allowed to override the clinical opinion of the psychiatrists when it is suggested that a patient could be cared for in less restricted surroundings. It is also the case that Tribunals relating to restricted patients are presided over by members of the judiciary who are from the same professional group as those who made the Restriction Orders in the first place.

It has been suggested that Section 73 should be amended to enable a MHRT to order the transfer or trial leave of a restricted patient where a bed is available for that patient at another hospital.

The Home Office, of course, could continue under these arrangements to have the right to attend Tribunals in matters that particularly concerned them but this change would allow clinicians to treat mentally disordered offenders more flexibly whilst still ensuring that the consent either of the Home Office or of the MHRT would be obtained before a move could take place. The Commission recognises that this is a controversial suggestion but it is a matter that many people feel needs discussion and debate.

(g) Section 117

At present arrangements for statutory aftercare apply only to those discharged from treatment sections. However, it is recognised that many patients discharged from Section 2 assessment orders are equally in need of aftercare. It is felt by many service staff that an extension of Section 117 to persons discharged from Section 2 would be in keeping with the Government's commitment to ensure that the care programme approach would be adhered to for this group of patients.

(h) Section 120

The Commission is sometimes approached by relatives about a complaint regarding someone detained under a guardianship order. At present the Commission has no remit to investigate complaints made by or on behalf of people under guardianship, nor does it visit or interview patients under guardianship. The Commission observes that many such patients are subject to considerable loss of their civil liberties, very often being de facto detained and would welcome an amendment to Section 120 to extend their remit to those under guardianship.

(i) Managers for the purpose of the Mental Health Act

The Commission is concerned about the statutory responsibility of Managers for detained patients in the growing number of private mental nursing homes and hospitals and are concerned that at present some Managers have a financial interest in the institution. The Commission would like to suggest that the following people should be precluded from becoming Managers under the Mental Health Act.

i. a person who has received or has an interest in the receipt of any payment on account of the maintenance of the patient;

ii. a practitioner on the staff of the Mental Nursing Home to which the patient is admitted;

(iii) the spouse, near relative, near connection by marriage or close business connection of either of those mentioned above.

12.
RACE AND CULTURE

12.1 Commission Structure and Organisation

The Commission's new structure includes a National Standing Committee on Race and Culture. The Commission's Policy on Race (Appendix 8) was accepted in February 1990 and its implementation is being monitored by the NSC. The Commission is pleased that its members now include a significant number of people from black and ethnic minorities and will be drawing the attention of ministers to the Policy on Race so that consideration can be given to the appointment of ethnic members to the Central Policy Committee of the Commission.

The NSC on Race and Culture held training days for members of the Commission in May 1991 and similar days are planned in future years.

12.2 Liaison with other Organisations

The Commission has supported the Commission for Racial Equality (CRE) in its efforts to examine alleged discrimination based on race in the allocation of treatment to psychiatric patients. The NSC on Race and Culture has had talks with the CRE on ethnic monitoring and a joint research project between the CRE and MHAC, to evaluate detention procedures under the Mental Health Act began in April 1991. This project which is based in a London borough, is expected to last about 18 months and will assist in developing advice for health authorities about the use of the Act and the care of detained patients from ethnic minority communities.

Other issues of concern relating to race and culture can be found in Chapters 3, 4, 5 and 6.

13.
CARE IN THE COMMUNITY

13.1 The Commission's Remit

The period under review has seen the publication of many reports and circulars setting out in greater detail the Government's intentions for Community Care, in particular its expectations of SSDs and the involvement of private and voluntary sector provision. The requirements of the NHS and Community Care Act 1990 and the White Paper 'Caring for People', although delayed in their implementation, set a demanding timetable for all agencies involved in the 'mixed economy of care'.

The Commission has welcomed this long overdue commitment to a comprehensively structured, nationwide community care programme and is concerned to see how it is actually brought into effect at a time when the statutory agencies concerned are subject to so many other organisational and functional changes. The Commission's interest in this area is focused primarily on the implementation of Section 117 of the Mental Health Act which relates to the provision of after-care to detained patients.

To this end the Commission has issued to all its members a standardised review schedule so that at each visit, after-care policies, multi-disciplinary working, care programming and review are discussed on a standardised basis. Early indications are that many authorities have made good progress but that a significant minority, usually those subject to extensive resource cuts through Community Charge capping are making slow headway.

Some authorities seem to have lost impetus and a sense of direction before basic frameworks have been agreed, especially where there are problems of liaison and joint operation with Health Service Trusts and/or in the communicating linkages between the purchaser and provider arms of both Local Authorities and Health Authorities. Lack of clarity about who should take on lead agency status in such organisationally complex situations can be difficult for the participants to determine. The process is at some risk of becoming hampered by even greater structural issues such as local government reorganisation, Community Charge reform and an approaching General Election.

13.2 Planning and Co-ordination of Effective Care and After-care

The Commission's concern in reviewing these multidimensional issues at local level is of course to see whether communication and joint working between all the parties involved is serving the interests of detained patients and their families now and for the future. In recent local discussions several points have emerged. For example the future role of the voluntary sector is a matter of concern in the new context, and in particular, whether voluntary organisations are actively involved in community care planning and review. Similarly, who can and should represent private sector interests and concerns? The White Paper emphasises the need to support informal carers, whose representatives often refer to the need for respite care for families of people with chronic disorders.

There are also concerns that elements of the Mental Health service may be provided by a variety of Trusts and Provider units, thus moving away from the ethos of a comprehensive service within a catchment area of a DHA. The Mental Health Service could then become fragmented and patients may have to travel to a neighbouring authority, which could make planning delivery and review almost impossibly complicated in individual cases.

Hospital provision is visibly shrinking — community alternatives are often too small and inadequate to cope with hospital closures. Many authorities are starting from a low base, and are looking to the voluntary and private sector to provide accommodation. This may mean that patients are placed long distances from their home. There are particular problems in resources for those with behaviour management problems and for people with long standing mental disabilities who are unable to care for themselves. RSUs are reluctant to take patients from Special Hospitals unless a community place can be promised and lack of suitable facilities is keeping patients in Special Hospitals.

There has been progress in the development of Community Teams for mentally handicapped people (CCMHT) but teams for mental health are comparatively rare. Respite care provision for mentally handicapped people is greater than for mentally ill people.

There is a lack of 'drop in' facilities especially out of normal working hours, at weekends and Bank Holidays. Where hostels exist, there is usually slow movement through them. Local Authority housing offered to people with mental health problems is often of poor quality and in rundown areas.

There is a need for greater co-operation between Health Authorities and Local Authorities providing Day facilities. In some instances there appears to be duplication of activities in day provision. Lack of community facilities result in discharged patients returning to hospital day facilities when community support would be more appropriate and finally there are very few employment opportunities.

13.3 Multi-Disciplinary Working

The Code of Practice encourages a strong multi-disciplinary approach to decision making from the point of assessment for admission, through to the decision making within the process of preparing After Care for the detained patient.

During the last two years Commissioners have drawn authorities' attention to situations where there has been a clear need to introduce a locally based multi-disciplinary approach. For example in some cases ASWs have appeared isolated from other professionals.

Many good examples of multi-disciplinary working have been identified. For example:

a. A day service which, through joint working, makes optimum use of facilities and breaks down barriers so clients do not feel they are restricted only to their day centre.

b. A team providing both preventive and aftercare services which includes family aides who provide invaluable practical assistance to people at a time when the practicalities of daily life can be very stressful.

c. St Helens Metropolitan Borough has been sectorised into four areas with a consultant having a key medical role in each area. Work is focused on community based multi-disciplinary based Resource Centres in each area. In-patient psychiatric provision is linked with the appropriate area, so that Community Nurses, Hospital Nurses, Social Workers, other therapists and medics work closely together on a strong multi-disciplinary basis. A Crisis Intervention Service is provided at one Resource base, with an overnight facility for those who need support.

13.4 Section 117 After Care: Care Programme Approach and Alternatives to Hospitalisation

Commissioners have noted with pleasure that most Health Authorities and Social Services Departments have completed their policies and procedures for the implementation of Section 117 of the Act. Most of those reviewed by the Commission have incorporated formats relating to services available generally, and those arranged for each individual patient/client. Actual implementation of Section 117 After Care can however prove extremely difficult in many places where resources are overstretched or limited in their ability to respond flexibly to special needs.

It is imperative that agreements for After Care provision identify those services which are needed as part of the "package of care" but which are not available. A common factor in problems of inappropriate After Care packaging results from sparsity in the range of local After Care Services.

There can, of course, be no compulsion associated with the implementation of S117, but questions are posed as to how many patients fail to take up the services on offer. There may be links between this failure rate and the re-admission rates to hospital.

Problems identified by the Commission in relation to section 117 include:

a. Inadequate record systems to identify who is entitled to receive after care and to monitor individual and collective use of services, including:

  i. whether objectives for the provision of support are being met and whether ther services can be discontinued

  ii. variations in the take up of services

  iii. the proportion of staff time spent in joint discussions about aftercare plans

  iv. problems caused by the lack of co-terminosity of Health and Local Authority boundaries

b. Some areas are involving voluntary agencies in a positive way in both planning and providing support to people after discharge from hospital, but the extent to which after care is recognised as a joint responsibility of Social Services, the Health Authority and voluntary agencies varies widely.

Community based mental health services providing aftercare under Section 117 to detained patients need to become much more sensitive to the different needs of cultural groups within the population. In a few places, special community services have been developed, often by the voluntary sector, to meet the needs of black people. A good example of a service designed for Asian women was discussed with Commissioners on a visit to a Midlands SSD; another example is the Harambee Housing project in Birmingham which is designed to meet the needs of Afro-Caribbeans with mental health problems.

Some examples of good practice in community mental health services are described below:

i. A resource centre providing 24 hour support, home treatment and a flexible response to individual's needs.

ii. A facility which provides for up to 11 short term emergency referrals and 30 day care places is considered to be both a model for future community care developments and to serve as an effective alternative to hospital admission.

iii. A hostel and day care facility providing counselling and a haven, particularly for women, and which is thought to have prevented unnecessary hospital admissions. It has also established a group for Asian women which was praised. However, it had been expected to serve as a crises intervention centre, but was not staffed at a level to achieve this. It was felt that a chance to provide crisis intervention and an alternative to hospital admission was being lost through inadequate resourcing.

13.5 Private and Voluntary Sector Care

This sector has undoubtedly contributed the majority of new places in community care, particularly for elderly people, without which hospital closures and social services care programmes could not proceed. Choices within the "mixed economy of care" are much wider than hitherto — for patients, carers and placing agencies concerned with older patients.

However constraints on Health Authority and Local Authority capital and revenue funding are hampering the capacity to provide the core infrastructure of specialised treatment, care, advice and support which community based caring agencies need. Gaps are particularly evident in the care of behaviourally disturbed patients, for mentally handicapped people with mental illnesses and personality disorders, and for people requiring secure or semi-secure accommodation. The resulting pressures on acute admission units and in special hospitals and RSUs are evident.

Some proprietors have grasped the opportunity to fill gaps in the market, but not always successfully. The Commission has needed to give special attention and make increased visits to several such units. The main concerns have been isolation from supportive infrastructure; staff levels, experience and training; availability of expert medical supervision; tendencies for placing authorities to wash their hands of problem patients.

Some private homes and voluntary agencies, particularly housing associations, though willing to help people with mental disorders, lack the skills or facilities to cope with problems which arise, but find that SSD community workers set limits on their intervention. Breakdowns of placement can result, even where the agency would wish to carry on. In such situations the planning of individual care programmes must not create false expectations of the help which will actually be given in times of crisis. A housing association manager summed up the situation: "we get any amount of care planning, but actual help often runs short, and most of all after five and at the weekend."

13.6 Detained Patients in Private Mental Nursing Homes

The Commission's remit applies to those nursing homes registered to take clients detained under the MHA, detained patients on leave and also formerly detained patients receiving after-care under Section 117. A considerable number of previously detained patients have moved into private sector care on discharge, notably elderly people with mental infirmity, mentally impaired people, and those with long-term mental illnesses. Relatively few visits are made to these homes, because of the Commission's limited resources, but greater priority should be given to visiting these people, and to closer collaborative working with the "arms length" inspection staff of HAs and SSDs. It is important to emphasize that mental nursing homes providing secure care for detained patients are visited by the Commission frequently. Kneesworth House in Cambridgeshire now provides care for the largest concentration of detained patients in England and Wales after the special hospitals.

Problems identified by the Commission include:

a. Keeping up to date with the rapid growth of such provision.

b. Statistics relating to detained patients who have moved into Private Nursing Homes on discharge should be obtainable from DHAs, but records were not always completed prior to implementation of the Care Programme Approach in April 1991.

c. Patients discharged from Hospital to one Nursing Home may move to another Nursing Home within weeks.

d. Some HAs have not been aware that Nursing Homes receiving detained patients must be registered for the purpose.

e. Rehabilitative training and expert support can be very limited for detained patients who are living in Mental Nursing Homes or residential homes whilst on Section 17 Leave. These concerns are acute in relation to patients from the Scott Clinic in homes in Wallasey on Merseyside and for patients from Ashworth Hospital in residential homes registered by local authorities.

f. Who the "Mental Health Act Managers" are, especially in relation to the exercise of Section 20 (renewal of authority to detain) and Section 23 (discharge) of the 1983 Mental Health Act.

g. Whether staff in the private sector understand the statutory rights of patients to information under Section 132 of the MHA.

h. Some patients repeatedly return to hospital following discharges to private sector care because of insufficient support to private homes from health and Social Services' community nursing staff. In some instances such support is actually embargoed by the Authorities concerned.

i. Some patients have been transferred for economic reasons to Homes at some distance from where they live. Sometimes Homes have admitted clients with no information about their background or needs.

In so far as it is relevant to the implementation of Section 117 of the Act the Commission will focus more attention on formerly detained patients in the private and voluntary sectors. Increased systematic monitoring of developments in this sector will enable more substantial observations to be made in the next Biennial Report.

13.7 Social Service Departments

The Commission has continued to encourage SSDs to give priority to mental health services. Shortages, and in some cases, reductions in resources are a cause of evident concern to all concerned, despite the introduction of Mental Health Specific Grants. Paradoxically, these uncertainties are evident at a time when national dictates on Care in the Community are ensuring that for the first time all Authorities are making plans and policies in a prescribed manner.

Amongst the issues that have arisen from the Commission regular meetings with social services departments are the following:

(a) Approved Social Workers (ASWs)

In general appreciation of the qualities of judgement and action by ASWs in the eyes of other professions involved in statutory procedures is now higher than in the past. This is a welcome testimony to the standards of selection and quality of training they receive.

(b) Recruitment and Training

Many London Boroughs have difficulty in the recruitment and retention of ASWs due to competing incentives offered by neighbouring authorities and the number of such staff who are promoted to managerial positions. A number of very successful consortia have been formed for initial training but refresher training is often lacking. In those authorities where locum cover is not provided, staff absences on training can create peer group pressures which deter candidates.

Training for staff who have the most intensive contact with clients — in day and residential services — is generally insufficient and may deteriorate further following the abandonment of the Certificate in Social Service training programme.

(c) Ethnic and Cultural Issues

Ethnic and cultural issues vary between areas but there are general problems in obtaining interpreters, particularly in areas where ethnic minorities are not well presented. This can lead to inappropriate admission and inadequate allocation of support services.

Difficulties in recruitment and retention of black ASWs are widely reported. Special aftercare provision for Afro Caribbean people appear scarce and there are continuing concerns regarding the high incidence of detention of young black men.

Some authorities have mentioned that they have difficulty in attracting Afro-Caribbean and Asian clients. This may be related to the low numbers of black staff, the inadequacy of cultural awareness by staff, the lack of appropriate religious services for black and ethnic groups. These issues have been raised at Commission meeting with SSDs and it is hoped that the next Biennial Report will be able to report progress in the addressing of their problems by local authorities.

Appropriate translation and cultural interpretation continue to be needed in Welsh speaking communities and by monitoring groups such as Irish people and travellers. The deficiencies can in many instances be appropriately rectified in consultation and co-operation with the minorities themselves.

(d) Out-of-Hours Cover

Out-of-hours cover is now almost universally provided by special teams, responsible for emergency support to all client groups. In a number of localities team members are specialising in mental health or child care responsibilities, a tendency which may increase as child care law reforms take effect. The Commission will be interested to see if such specialisation affects the quality of liaison with other agencies and with day time services, which has been criticised in previous Biennial Reports.

(e) Personal Safety

The Commission welcomes the fact that training in personal safety and in the management of disturbed and dangerous behaviours are becoming increasingly widespread. It has noted that in some localities, mostly inner cities, mental health emergency requests are responded to by staff in pairs. The increased use of communications and information technology, particularly by out of hours staff, appears to be valuable.

13.8 Section 136

Previous Biennial Reports have recorded concerns about the lack of policies, procedures and in-service training in many Police Forces. There have also been comments on the poorly co-ordinated support provided by health and social services workers to Police on the ground, particularly out of hours. In some places, notably inner cities these criticisms must be restated despite the powerful guidance in the Code of Practice about the importance of agreed local policies and procedure.

It is still the practice in some localities for constables to take persons apparently showing signs of mental illness from a public place to a Police Station, where a senior officer will decide if transfer to a place of safety in a hospital should be arranged.

Arrangements which reduce the stress and disturbance which so often attends these incidents are now operating in many areas. In Tower Hamlets a Police Inspector goes to the point of contact in the community and makes an on the spot decision, perhaps avoiding removal to a Police Station. In Taunton duty social workers attend all crises in which the Police consider that mental illness is a factor. There have been several well thought out revisions of local policy and practice, for example in Hampshire, which could now be widely used as models.

13.9 Guardianship

The Third Biennial Report commented 'In the next two years the Commission will continue to contribute to the clarification of the policy and professional issues surrounding the use of Guardianship and it will continue to encourage ASWs and Local Authorities to give its use active consideration.'

Despite this, the statistics for Guardianship give the impression that it is little used. Few Departments have a written policy, and where they do, express continuing reservations about the usefulness and effectiveness of this provision in the Act. Many social workers feel that the three specific powers given by the Act to Guardians are unenforceable without the co-operation of the client, and there are no sanctions for non-compliance. They argue that if clients are willing to co-operate, Guardianship is not necessary, or may indeed be an unethical restraint on individual freedom. It appears to be used mainly to determine a place of residence, most often for elderly or mentally impaired people. It has to form part of a treatment plan, and when the client has settled in, Guardianship should be lifted wherever possible.

The lack of powers to convey patients has widely been cited as the major constraint on the effectiveness of Guardianship, and in one County the number of patients fell from 40 to 20 when staff learned that this power did not exist. Subsequently the number has risen again, as staff have learned legitimate ways of negotiating co-operation with patients. There appears to be widespread agreement, however, that an amendment to the Act is needed to grant such a power to guardians and at its April 1991 conference the Commission agreed to make such a recommendation to Ministers. (For further discussion see the next section and see also Chapter 11).

13.10 Community Treatment Orders (CTOs)

In the third Biennial Report (Sections 11.3, 12.9) the Commission reported on the work it had undertaken to consider the arguments for and against the creation of a CTO. The steps taken to promote discussion were outlined, acknowledging the philosophical, ethical and practical issues involved.

The discussion has continued, and the Commission has produced further papers, outlining various possible ways forward. Concern has continued to centre on the aftercare of detained patients, the use of guardianship, ways of preventing relapse and re-admission to hospital, and whether a CTO would promote the welfare of patients. The increasing changes in the development of the pattern of care from large institutions to small community settings has prompted the Commission to re-examine the issues in the period under review.

On its visits to health and Social Services Authorities Commissioners are asked frequently to express a view and it became clear that the time had come to reach a conclusion. The Commission's NSC on Community Care was asked to consider the issues and make recommendations to the Commission. Several choices were outlined and discussed by the Commission at its Conference in York in April 1991.

The Commission decided by a majority vote, that at present there is not enough evidence to indicate that a CTO is needed, but it will monitor future developments and encourage research. Meanwhile it will press for the increased use of guardianship, which appears to be held back by the lack of a power to convey. This has seriously hindered the constructive use of this power.

As reported in the previous section, in some Authorities the number of guardianship orders has decreased dramatically, once they become aware of the lack of a power to convey. Guardianship can be particularly useful in providing a framework for residential or day care as fear of change may prevent people from accepting options which could improve the quality of their lives. It could be a means of persuading the persuadable. The Commission therefore urges the Secretary of State for Health to consider extending the Powers of the Guardian to include the power to convey. This would not include powers to admit to hospitals or administer medication.

14.
THE NHS AND COMMUNITY CARE ACT 1990

14.1 Introduction

The Commission has reviewed its policies and procedures in the light of the major changes now taking place in the National Health Service and Local Authority Social Services Departments as a result of the NHS and Community Care Act, 1990. The Commission's remit remains of course unchanged and its responsibility to the Secretaries of State to oversee the implementation of the Act and monitor the care and treatment of detained patients refers to all such patients in England and Wales, whether detained in NHS directly managed hospital units, NHS Trusts or independent sector hospitals and registered mental nursing homes. The Commission believes that the changes provide opportunities for the Commission to enhance its influence on the services provided for detained patients through the new arrangements. Some concerns have been expressed to the Commission about the impact of the new arrangements on the working of the Mental Health Act which are addressed in this chapter.

14.2 Managers duties under the Act

Managers for the Mental Health Act were formerly drawn largely from the non-executive members of District Health Authorities, although many Authorities invited co-opted members to participate in this work. Now that there are only 5 non-executive members on each Health Authority or Trust Board the majority of Managers are not members of the Authority or Trust but co-opted to a sub-committee of the Authority or Trust. It is heartening to report that many former Health Authority members with a good deal of knowledge and experience of the Act have agreed to continue this work on behalf of new Authorities and Trusts, but in many instances new Managers are in place who require training. There have been delays reported in Managers' hearing appeals and the Commission continues to remind Managers that this work must be given priority. It is however pleasing to note that Managers are now usually in attendance at meetings following Commission visits, a trend which is greatly welcomed.

The Commission recommends that one Manager at least should be a non-executive member of the responsible Health Authority or Trust Board.

14.3 Service agreements

The Commission does not propose to issue detailed guidance on the content of service agreements between purchasing authorities and provider units, since arrangements for the care and treatment of detained patients are a matter for the purchasing authority alone to specify. Nor will the Commission endorse proposed agreements. Nevertheless, the Commission will wish to look at service agreements on occasion in pursuit of its statutory responsibilities and in the investigation of complaints. The Commission intends to assist authorities by issuing guidance on the principles which should underlie the agreements made about services for detained patients which can be interpreted in the light of local circumstances.

14.4 Commission reports

It has been the Commission's practice to report the findings of Commission visiting teams to the Health Authority directly responsible for managing the unit visited. The Commission will in the future continue to address its reports to the managers responsible for *providing* the service but, will also copy relevant reports to *purchasing* authorities. The same practice will apply where relevant to reports of complaints investigations.

14.5 Role of Regional Health Authorities (RHAs)

The Commission is conscious of the changing role of RHAs and note that many are divesting themselves of direct management responsibility of specialist services, for example forensic psychiatry services. The Commission recognises, however, that Regions have an enhanced role to monitor the performance of purchasing District Health Authorities in fulfilling Regions' strategies for all mental health services. The Commission will therefore seek to develop an appropriate relationship with Regions to ensure that the needs of detained patients are met.

15.
THE COMMISSION AND RESEARCH

The Commission has long recognised the contribution that competent research can make to proper understanding, not only of how the Mental Health Act works, but also to improving the provision of care to, and safeguard of the rights of, detained patients. The Commission has also recognised that in carrying out its statutory responsibility it has acquired a substantial amount of information that could usefully be the subject of high quality academic research, the results of which could greatly assist the Commission in effectively carrying out its responsibilities. Consequent upon centralisation the Commission has established a Research and Information NSC, part of whose functions is to oversee the Commission involvement in research. It is important to emphasize that the Commission has no budget to support research projects and that it has no intention of becoming involved in the management of research projects. The NSC has a membership of Commissioners drawn from a multidisciplinary background and in relation to research proposals that involve the use of the Commission's own data it will act as the Commission equivalent of a local Research Ethics Committee (augmented where necessary by external members).

The Commission has identified three ways in which the Commission will become involved in research:

a. Approaches will be made to the Commission by researchers seeking approval for research proposals which are concerned with matters that fall within the Commission remit (for example, the apparently disproportionate high number of compulsory admission to one particular hospital as compared to other hospitals drawing from the same catchment area). In these circumstances the Commission will confine itself to indicating whether it judges the issues which are the subject of the proposals warrant such research.

b. The Commission will be approached by researchers seeking to use Commission data. For example the Commission has agreed to a recent proposal to examine the early history of the Commission and the production of the Mental Health Act Code of Practice. Another research project shortly to get underway will examine aspects of the operation of Part IV of the Mental Health Act relating to the consent to treatment safeguards. All such proposals will be considered by the relevant Research and Information NSC in its capacity as the Commissions Research Ethics Committee and it will have to be satisfied that the proposal is ethically acceptable in accordance with the guidelines shortly to be issued to all Health Authorities and NHS Trusts by the NHS Management Executive.

c. The Commission will from time to time identify issues relevant to its statutory remit which will benefit from research. For example, an increase in a use of Mental Health Act sections in parts of the London area has been identified and at the time of going to press it appears that funding will be obtained for researchers at Loughborough University to undertake the project.

The Commissions involvement in research on matters relevant to its remit in the manner described above, will hopefully be of value not only to the Commission but perhaps more importantly to detained patients and those with responsibility for the care of their health and observation of their rights.

16.
COLLABORATION AND CONTACT WITH OTHER AGENCIES

The Commission does not undertake its statutory responsibility in a vacuum. All its activities take place within the general framework of the provision of Mental Health care and of the agencies and professionals involved in the delivery of such care. The framework is becoming increasingly complicated and the Commission regards it as particularly important that it maintains effective dialogue with relevant agencies and professional bodies in pursuit of its statutory responsibilities.

During the period under review and especially after centralisation more effective contact has been established with a number of bodies. The Commission and the National Association of Health Authorities and Trusts are to hold a joint conference in November 1991 entitled "The Mental Health Act and Nursing Homes" for Health Authority personnel involved with registration under Mental Health Act 1984 and personnel for mental nursing homes. Contact has also been renewed with the Association of Community Health Councils and the Greater London Association of Community Health Councils with a view to collaboration.

In the Third Biennial Report the Commission was critical of the lack of secure facilities in Wales. The Commission was therefore, delighted to collaborate with the Department of Forensic Psychiatric Services, based at Whitchurch Hospital, in planning an important conference to take place November 1991 about services for difficult to manage patients in Wales.

Although the Commission and Mental Health Review Tribunals are separate organisations with different functions (the Commission as a matter of policy does not get involved in complaints about the conduct of tribunal hearings) both in a general sense have extensive experience of issues relating to aspects of detained patients lives which they can usually share. Whilst the present structure of the tribunals make contact difficult, the Commission's Chief Executive has welcomed the opportunity to address a number of meetings of tribunal members around the country about the role of the Commission and areas of possible collaboration. The Commission hopes that such opportunities to collaborate will increase.

During the period under review there have been a number of useful meetings with various regional inspectorates of the Social Services which have also on occasion made a contribution to the development of the Commission response to particular issues arising out of visits to hospitals and meetings with Social Services Departments. Early in 1991 a meeting took place between officers of Social Services Inspectorate London Region, the Commission and the Metropolitan Police where the revised police procedures on the implementation of Section 136 were constructively discussed.

The Commission is one of a number of agencies involved in different ways with the inspection and monitoring of Health and Social Services. Previous Biennial Reports have referred to the importance of such bodies being aware of each others respective areas of responsibility and also of the need to ensure that the providers of Mental Health Care are not unnecessarily diverted from their primary case work by an avoidable close sequence of events from a variety of such agencies. Generally where this situation arises the Commission is advised by the unit to be visited and where appropriate the Commission will be as amenable as possible in changing its scheduled visit to a more convenient date. The Commission is however aware that there could usefully be greater contact between the various inspection bodies about a range of relevant matters and to this end a meeting is planned with the Audit Commission and a higher level of contact will be established with other relevant agencies.

17.
THE COMMISSION'S RESPONSE TO CONSULTATION DOCUMENTS

In Chapter 2 it was pointed out that one of the objectives of centralisation was to enable the Commission to have a greater influence at a more general level on policy issues which are relevant to its statutory responsibilities. Such an objective in no way implies that the Commission was negligent in this regard prior to centralisation, rather, that this task, given the increased staff resources and the establishment of the NSCs, will be more effectively carried out. The full value of these changes has yet to be felt as priorities had to be given during the process of centralisation to ensuring that the undertaking of the Commission basic functions was maintained. Responsibility for visiting detained patients, dealing with complaints and monitoring the consent to treatment provisions of the Act was disrupted as little as possible. The Commission has however, been able to comment upon a number of important documents including Home Office Circular 66/90 (Provision for Mentally Disordered Offenders), the Home Office Efficiency Scrutiny of the Prison Medical Service, the Law Commission's consultation document on the mentally incapacitated adults and decision making (see Chapter 11) and the draft revised guidance from the Department of Health/NHS Executive on doctors approved under Section 12 of the Act. In addition the Commission submitted evidence to Lord Justice Woolf's Inquiry into Prison Disturbances (see Chapter 9).

As the benefits of centralisation become more apparent it is hoped that the Commission will be able to make even more effective use of its practical experience of monitoring the operation of the Mental Health Act by contributing appropriately to discussion of relevant policy issues.

APPENDIX 1

EXTRACTS FROM MENTAL HEALTH ACT 1983

General protection of detained patients

120.—(1) The Secretary of State shall keep under review the exercise of the powers and the **1-128** discharge of the duties conferred or imposed by this Act so far as relating to the detention of patients or to patients liable to be detained under this Act and shall make arrangements for persons authorised by him in that behalf—

    (a) to visit and interview in private patients detailed under this Act in hospitals and mental nursing homes; and

    (b) to investigate—

        (i) any complaint made by a person in respect of a matter that occurred while he was detained under this Act in a hospital or mental nursing home and which he considers has not been satisfactorily dealt with by the managers of that hospital or mental nursing home; and

        (ii) any other complaint as to the exercise of the powers or the discharge of the duties conferred or imposed by this Act in respect of a person who is or has been so detained.

(2) The arrangements made under this section in respect of the investigation of complaints may exclude matters from investigation in specified circumstances and shall not require any person exercising functions under the arrangements to undertake or continue with any investigation where he does not consider it appropriate to do so.

(3) Where any such complaint as is mentioned in subsection (1)(b)(ii) above is made by a Member of Parliament and investigated under the arrangements made under this section the results of the investigation shall be reported to him.

(4) For the purpose of any such review as it mentioned in subsection (1) above or of carrying out his functions under arrangements made under this section any person authorised in that behalf by the Secretary of State may at any reasonable time—

    (a) visit and interview and, if he is a registered medical practitioner, examine in private any patient in a mental nursing home; and

    (b) require the production of and inspect any records relating to the detention or treatment of any person who is or has been detained in a mental nursing home.

(5) [*Repealed by the Registered Homes Act* 1984, *s.*57(3), *Sched.* 3.]

(6) The Secretary of State may make such provision as he may with the approval of the Treasury determine for the payment of remuneration allowances, pensions or gratuities to or in respect of persons exercising functions in relation to any such review as is mentioned in subsection (1) above or functions under arrangements made under this section.

Mental Health Act Comission

121.—(1) Without prejudice to section 126(3) of the National Health Service Act 1977 (powers to **1-129** vary or revoke orders or directions) there shall continue to be a special health authority known as the Mental Health Act Commission established under section 11 of that Act.

(2) Without prejudice to the generality of his powers under section 13 of that Act, the Secretary of State shall direct the Commission to perform on his behalf—

    (a) the function of appointing registered medical practitioners for the purposes of Part IV of this Act and section 118 above and of appointing other persons for the purposes of section 57(2)(a) above; and

    (b) the functions of the Secretary of State under sections 61 and 120(1) and (4) above.

(3) The registered medical practitioners and other persons appointed for the purposes mentioned in subsection (2)(a) above may include members of the Commission.

(4) The Secretary of State may, at the request of or after consultation with the Commission and after consulting such other bodies as appear to him to be concerned, direct the Commission to keep under review the care and treatment, or any aspect of the care and treatment, in hospitals and mental nursing homes of patients who are not liable to be detained under this Act.

(5) For the purpose of any such review as is mentioned in subsection (4) above any person authorised in that behalf by the Commission may at any reasonable time—

    (a) visit and interview and, if he is a registered medical practitioner, examine in private any patient in a mental nursing home; and (*b*) require the production of and inspect any records relating to the treatment of any person who is or has been a patient in a mental nursing home.

(6) The Secretary of State may make such provision as he may with the approval of the Treasury determine for the payment of remuneration, allowances, pensions or gratuities to or in respect of persons exercising functions in relation to any such review as is mentioned in subsection (4) above.

(7) The Commission shall review any decision to withhold a postal packet (or anything contained in it) under subsection (1)(*b*) or (2) of section 134 below if an application in that behalf is made—

(*a*) in a case under subsection (1)(*b*), by the patient; or

(*b*) in a case under subsection (2), either by the patient or by the person by whom the postal packet was sent;

and any such application shall be made within six months of the receipt by the applicant of the notice referred to in subsection (6) of that section.

(8) On an application under subsection (7) above the Commission may direct that the postal packet which is the subject of the application (or anything contained in it) shall not be withheld and the managers in question shall comply with any such direction.

(9) The Secretary of State may by regulations make provision with respect to the making and determination of applications under subsection (7) above, including provision for the production to the Commission of any postal packet which is the subject of such an application.

(10) The Commission shall in the second year after its establishment and subsequently in every second year publish a report on its activities; and copies of every such report shall be sent by the Commission to the Secretary of State who shall lay a copy before each House of Parliament.

(11) Paragraph 9 of Schedule 5 to the said Act of 1977 (pay and allowances for chairmen and members of health authorities) shall have effect in relation to the Mental Health Act Commission as if references in sub-paragraphs (1) and (2) to the Chairman included references to any member and as if sub-paragraphs (4) and (5) were omitted.

DEFINITIONS
  "Hospital": s.145(1).
  "Mental nursing home": s.145(1).
  "Patient": s.145(1).

TRANSITIONAL PROVISION
  Sched. 5, para. 5.

1983 No. 892

NATIONAL HEALTH SERVICE, ENGLAND AND WALES

The Mental Health Act Commission (Establishment and Constitution) Order 1983

Made - - - -	*17th June* 1983
Laid before Parliament	*1st July* 1983
Coming into Operation	
Articles 1, 2 and 4	*1st September* 1983
Remainder	*30th September* 1983

The Secretary of State for Social Services, in exercise of the powers conferred upon him by section 11 of the National Health Service Act 1977(**a**), and of all other powers enabling him in that behalf, hereby makes the following order:

Citation, commencement and interpretation

1.—(1) This order may be cited as the Mental Health Act Commission (Establishment and Constitution) Order 1983 and shall come into operation on 1st September 1983 except that Article 3 shall come into operation on 30th September 1983.

(2) In this order—

"the Act" means the Mental Health Act 1983(**b**);

"the Commission" means the Commission established by Article 2 of this Order.

Establishment of the Commission

2. There is hereby established a special health authority which shall be known as the Mental Health Act Commission.

Functions of the Commission

3.—(1) Subject to and in accordance with such directions as the Secretary of State may give to the Commission, the Commission shall, in addition to performing its functions specified in the Act, perform on behalf of the Secretary of State the functions specified in paragraph (2) of this Article and such other functions as the Secretary of State may direct.

(**a**) 1977 c. 49; section 11(1) was amended by the Health Services Act 1980 (c. 53), Schedule 1, paragraph 31.
(**b**) 1983 c. 20.

[H83/1180]

(2) The functions of the Secretary of State referred to in paragraph (1) above are—

(*a*) the function of appointing registered medical practitioners for the purposes of Part IV of the Act (consent to treatment) and section 118 of the Act (practitioners required to certify consent and to give second opinion) and of appointing other persons for the purposes of section 57(2)(*a*) of the Act (persons required to certify consent);

(*b*) the functions of the Secretary of State under section 61 of the Act (review of treatment);

(*c*) the functions of the Secretary of State under section 120(1) and (4) of the Act (general protection of patients detained under the Act); and

(*d*) the function of submitting to the Secretary of State proposals as to the content of the code of practice which he shall prepare, and from time to time revise, under section 118(1) of the Act, and in particular to propose, for the purposes of section 118(2) of the Act, forms of medical treatment in addition to any specified in regulations made for the purposes of section 57 of the Act which in the opinion of the Commission give rise to special concern.

Constitution of the Commission

4. The Commission shall consist of such number of members as the Secretary of State may from time to time determine of whom one shall be the chairman and one the vice-chairman.

Norman Fowler,
Secretary of State for Social Services.

17th June 1983.

EXPLANATORY NOTE

(This Note is not part of the Order.)

This Order provides for the establishment, as required by section 56(1) of the Mental Health (Amendment) Act 1982 (c. 51), and the constitution of a special health authority, to be known as the Mental Health Act Commission, to exercise functions under the Mental Health Act 1983, including the appointment of medical practitioners and other persons for the purposes of that Act, the review of treatment, the general protection of patients detained under that Act and the submission to the Secretary of State of proposals for the preparation and revision of a Code of Practice.

1983 No. 894

NATIONAL HEALTH SERVICE, ENGLAND AND WALES

The Mental Health Act Commission Regulations 1983

Made - - - - -	*17th June* 1983
Laid before Parliament	*1st July* 1983
Coming into Operation	*1st September* 1983

The Secretary of State for Social Services, in exercise of the powers conferred upon him by paragraph 12 of Schedule 5 to the National Health Service Act 1977**(a)**, and of all other powers enabling him in that behalf, hereby makes the following regulations:—

Citation, commencement and interpretation

1.—(1) These regulations may be cited as the Mental Health Act Commission Regulations 1983 and shall come into operation on 1st September 1983.

(2) In these regulations, unless the context otherwise requires—

"the Commission" means the Mental Health Act Commission established by the Order;

"the Order" means the Mental Health Act Commission (Establishment and Constitution) Order 1983**(b)**.

Appointment of chairman and members

2. The chairman and members of the Commission shall be appointed by the Secretary of State.

Tenure of office of chairman and members

3. Subject to the following provisions of these regulations and to any provisions of regulations applied by these regulations, the term of office of the chairman or a member shall be such period, not exceeding four years, as the Secretary of State may specify on making the appointment.

Termination of tenure of office

4.—(1) The chairman or a member of the Commission may resign his office at any time during the period for which he was appointed by giving notice in writing to the Secretary of State.

(a) 1977 c. 49.

(b) S.I. 1983/892.

[H83-1181]

(2) Notwithstanding that the appointment of the chairman or any member is for a term of years, the Secretary of State may, at any time, terminate that person's tenure of office.

Eligibility for re-appointment
5. Subject to any provisions of regulations applied by these regulations as to disqualification from membership, the chairman or a member of the Commission shall, on the termination of his tenure of office, be eligible for re-appointment.

Vice-chairman
6.—(1) The Secretary of State may appoint a member of the Commission to be vice-chairman for such period as the Secretary of State may specify on making the appointment.

(2) Where no such appointment is made, the chairman and members of the Commission shall elect one of their number, other than the chairman, to be vice-chairman for a period of one year or, where the period of his membership during which he is elected has less than a year to run, for the remainder of such period.

(3) Any member so appointed or elected may at any time resign from the office of vice-chairman by giving notice in writing—

(*a*) if he was appointed by the Secretary of State, to the Secretary of State;

(*b*) in any other case, to the chairman of the Commission,

and the Secretary of State may thereupon appoint another member or, failing such an appointment, the chairman and members shall thereupon elect another member as vice-chairman in accordance with paragraph (1) or, as the case may be, paragraph (2) of this regulation.

Committees and sub-committees
7.—(1) The Secretary of State shall appoint a central policy committee of the Commission, consisting wholly of members of the Commission, but the Commission may co-opt any other member of the Commission as a member of the committee.

(2) Subject to paragraph (3) of this regulation and subject to and in accordance with such directions as the Secretary of State may give to that committee, the central policy committee shall perform on behalf of the Commission the following functions:—

(*a*) the function mentioned in Article 3(2)(*d*) of the Order (proposals for the code of practice);

(*b*) the preparation of the report on the Commission's activities required by section 121(10) of the Mental Health Act 1983(**a**);

(*c*) any other function, or activity in connection with any function, which the Commission may require it to perform.

(**a**) S.I. 1983 c. 20.

2

(3) The functions mentioned in paragraph (2)(*a*) and (*b*) of this regulation, and any such function under paragraph (2)(*c*) of this regulation as the Commission may specify, shall be performed in consultation with the Commission.

(4) Subject to such directions as may be given by the Secretary of State, the Commission may, and if so directed shall, appoint committees of the Commission, consisting wholly of members of the Commission.

(5) A committee appointed under this regulation may, subject to such directions as may be given by the Secretary of State or the Commission, appoint sub-committees consisting wholly of members of the Commission.

(6) Any power in this regulation to appoint members of the Commission as members of any committee or sub-committee shall include the power to appoint the chairman as a member of such a committee or sub-committee.

Meetings and proceedings
8.—(1) The meetings and proceedings of the Commission shall be conducted in accordance with Standing Orders made under paragraph (2) of this regulation.

(2) Subject to paragraph (3) of this regulation, the Commission shall make, and may vary or revoke, Standing Orders for the regulation of their proceedings and business and provision may be made in those Standing Orders for the suspension of those Orders.

(3) The Standing Orders shall provide that there shall be held at least one full meeting of the Commission in any year.

Application of regulations relating to membership
9. The provisions of regulation 7 (disqualification for appointment) and regulation 8 (cessation of disqualification) of the National Health Service (Regional and District Health Authorities: Membership and Procedure) Regulations 1983**(a)** shall apply as if any reference in those regulations to an Authority included a reference to the Commission.

Norman Fowler,
Secretary of State for Social Services.

17th June 1983.

(a) S.I. 1983/315.

APPENDIX 2

NATIONAL STANDING COMMITTEES TERMS OF REFERENCE

Research and Information

1. To monitor and keep under review the Commission's arrangements for the storage and handling of information arising from its own work; and make proposals for its improvement.

2. To initiate proposals for research or monitoring activities, or receive them from within and outside the MHAC, and to comment upon them.

3. To oversee the collation of material for the preparation and publication of the Biennial Report.

4. To undertake other relevant tasks as are referred to it by the Commission, the CPC or the Chief Executive.

Visiting

1. To study the pattern of Commission visits to hospitals and to monitor such visits.

2. To develop procedures to improve the Commission's practice in undertaking this task.

3. To advise the Commission on issues arising out of undertaking visits where they are not better dealt with by another NSC.

4. To prepare material for the Biennial Report.

5. To undertake other relevant tasks referred to it by the Commission, CPC or the Chief Executive.

Mental handicap and non-volitional patients

1. To study and keep under review all aspects of the care and treatment of and services for people who are —
   (a) Mentally handicapped with psychiatric illness or who are behaviourally distrubed
   (b) Non-volitional patients.

2. To advise the Commission on issues relating to these groups of patients.

3. To contribute to the effective undertaking by the Commission of its statutory remit in relation to these groups of patients.

4. To prepare material for the Biennial Report.

5. To undertake all the relevant tasks referred to it by the Commission, CPC or the Chief Executive.

Legal and Parliamentary Affairs

1. To establish liaison with relevant parliamentary committees and/or MPs.

2. To monitor legal and parliamentary developments and activities that are relevant to the Commission's work.

3. To advise the Commission on legal problems with the 1983 Mental Health Act and related legislation.

4. To monitor legal "opinions/advice" given by the Commission and develop procedures to improve the practice of Commissioners and staff.

5. To prepare material for the Biennial Report.

6. To undertake other relevant tasks referred to it by the Commission, CPC or the Chief Executive.

Code of Practice

1. To keep under review the Commission's monitoring of the implementation of the Mental Health Act Code of Practice and contribute to the development of procedures to improve the practice of Commissioners in undertaking that task.

2. To advise the CPC and the Commission on issues relating to the meaning and application of the Code in particular any part of the Code that requires revision and in relation to which the Commission should consider making recommendations to the Secretary of State.

3. To prepare material for the Biennial Report.

4. To undertake other relevant tasks referred to it by the Commission, CPC or the Chief Executive.

Community Care

1. To study and keep under review the provision within the community of treatment and care to people with mental health problems.

2. To monitor Commission meetings with Social Service Departments and to develop procedures to improve the practices of the Commission in undertaking such tasks.

3. To advise the CPC and Commission on issues relating to community care.

4. To prepare relevant material for the Biennial Report.

5. To undertake other relevant tasks referred to it by the Commission, CPC or the Chief Executive.

Race and Culture

1. To study and report on issues of race and culture as they relate to the Commission's work.

2. To advise the CPC and the Commission on relevant issues and to contribute to the promotion of a greater understanding within the Commission of matters relevant to race and culture and the development of Commission policies, procedures and practice that reflects that understanding.

3. To monitor the implementation of any policy promulgated by and for the Commission and to make proposals for updating where necessary.

4. To prepare material for the Biennial Report.

5. To undertake other relevant tasks as referred to it by the Commission, CPC or the Chief Executive.

Mentally Disordered Offenders

1. To study and monitor the provisions for the care and treatment of and services for "difficult and offender patients" with mental health problems.

2. To advise the CPC and the Commission on issues or concern relating to this group of patients.

3. To contribute to the effective undertaking by the Commission of its statutory tasks in relation to this group of patients.

4. To prepare material for the Biennial Report.

5. To undertake other relevant tasks referred to it by the Commission, CPC or the Chief Executive.

Consent to Treatment

1. To monitor the Commission's undertaking of its responsibilities in relation to Part IV of the Mental Health Act 1983.

2. To develop procedures to improve practice in relation to the undertaking of such responsibilities.

3. To advise the CPC and the Commission on issues arising out of the undertaking of such responsibilities or which are otherwise relevant to consent to treatment generally.

4. To prepare material for the Biennial Report.

5. To undertake other relevant tasks as referred to it by the Commission, CPC or the Chief Executive.

Complaints

1. To monitor the Commission's investigation of complaints pursuant to Section 120(1)(b) and to develop procedures to improve the Commission's practice.

2. To advise the CPC and the Commission on issues of concern arising out of such activities where they are not better dealt with by another NSC.

3. To prepare material for the Biennial Report.

4. To undertake other relevant tasks as referred to it by the Commission, CPC or the Chief Executive.

APPENDIX 3

COMMISSION EXPENDITURE

	1989/90 £	1990/91 £	1987/89 £
Commission Fees & Expenses	619,042	714,305	1,198,000
Second opinion doctors Fees & Expenses	378,202	424,107	588,000
Staff Salaries	223,524	325,216	485,000
Non-manpower Expenditure	89,174	118,790	303,000
	1,359,942	1,582,418	2,574,000

APPENDIX 4

THE SPECIAL HOSPITAL VISITING POLICY

Aims and Objectives

The Commissions visiting programme for the Special Hospitals should:—

1. ensure that the rights and interests of Special Hospital patients are effectively safeguarded;

2. ensure that every patient in the Special Hospitals is contacted by Commissioners at least once a year;

3. be cost-effective within the resources allocated by CPC; and

4. be subject to consultation with the Special Hospitals Service Authority before adoption by the Commission.

Principles

The following principles are recommended:

5. Visiting Commissioners should relate to clinical units to facilitate communication with wards, nursing managers, responsible medical officers, and other clinical services.

6. The Commission should be organised to interact effectively with the clinical staff, the clinical teams, the Hospital Advisory Committees, the Hospital Management Teams and Special Hospitals Service Authority.

Practical Implementation

Special Hospital Panels.

7. All Commissioners should be expected to make a substantial commitment to the visiting programme for the Special Hospitals.

8. Each Commissioner should be allocated to one of the Special Hospital Panels (SHP), the number in each SHP being proportional to the number of patients in the Special Hospital for which they have responsibility. Each SHP will appoint a convenor.

9. A system should be established for determining the availability of Commissioners for Special Hospital visits, to synchronise with the visits to hospitals and meetings with social services departments carried out by Commission Visiting Teams.

10. A system should be devised for inducting new members of each SHP, including orientation visits to the relevant Special Hospital.

11. (a) It is the policy of the Commission to make "out of hours" and "unannounced" visits;
    (b) the relevant SHP convenors will decide when such visits should be made and shall inform the Chief Executive.

Visiting Team

12. Each SHP should be divided into visiting teams, depending upon the requirements of the units to be visited. Each visiting team should choose its own leader.

13. SHPs should meet at least on the occasion of each Commission meeting and review general issues in respect of the Special Hospital with which they are concerned. Each should make decisions as necessary, from time to time as to the composition of its teams and their allocation to units and responsibility in respect of particular departments and non-ward areas.

14. Each visiting team should be responsible for reviewing the documentation relating to the patient's detention, and for monitoring the implementation and recording of Part IV of the Act within its clinical units.

15. The visiting teams should also visit systematically non-ward areas as determined by their respective SHP's, e.g. rehabilitation workshops, schools, etc., according to an agreed protocol to ensure a consistent approach.

16. the visiting team should meet the clinical teams of the relevant clinical units at the closing meeting of the visit, unless there are special reasons for cancelling the final meeting. At such meetings, only issues which can be dealt with at ward level will be raised.

Team Convenors

17. Within the budget determined by the CPC the frequency of visiting to the units or wards of the Special Hospital should be decided by the team leaders for that hospital in conjunction with the SHP convenor.

18. Where it is thought necessary, the SHP convenor should ask CPC for an increased allocation of funded visiting days to meet special needs.

19. Each visiting team should consider the desirability both of out of hours and unannounced visits and if they think that such a visit is necessary, they should put a proposition for it through their leader to the convenor of the SHP.

20. The Team Leaders should meet at least once every six months other than at Commission meetings to share information, to monitor and evaluate the programme, to review complaints, to consider postal packets withheld, to prepare a report for the Hospital Management Team, to identify matters to be reported to the CPC and matters to be considered for the Biennial Report.

21. The formal meetings of the SHP should be supported by a member of staff.

22. The SHP convenor and complaints and visiting representatives of the SHP and visiting team leaders should meet with the HMT at least twice yearly.

23. Meetings at periodic intervals to be determined will also take place between each Hospital Advisory Committee and commissioners from the relevant SHP.

24. The SHP should identify matters to be discussed at the bianniel meeting between representatives of the Commission (including the Chairman) and the Special Hospitals Service Authority.

Clinical Units

25. To ensure that the visiting teams relate to appropriate clinical units, discussion should take place with the Hospital Management Team. The importance of the relationship with the responsible medical officer, and the other clinical staff should be stressed to ensure effective co-ordination in relation to transfer delays and consent to treatment issues.

26. To facilitate continuity of visiting, the hospital should be asked to notify the Commission when patients are transferred between wards, so that information on patients can be passed between visiting teams.

APPENDIX 5

COMPLAINTS POLICY

1. **The Statutory basis of the Commission's complaints remit**

   The statutory basis for the Commission's complaints remit is to be found at Section 120(1)(b) of the Act. There are two types of complaint that the Commission may investigate and guidance about them is set out in full in the guidelines (see paragraph 1 on page 10 in particular).

   Section 120(2) gives to the Commission the discretion not to investigate a complaint or to discontinue a complaint where it is appropriate to do so.

2. **Objectives of Complaints Policy**

   The aim of the Policy is to ensure that:

   (a) Complaints received by the Commission are properly identified as falling within or without Section 120;

   (b) Complaints are investigated promptly, effectively and fairly within a reasonable timescale (see paragraph 4 on page 4);

   (c) Where possible conciliation between Complainant and the individual organisation complained about is undertaken and a settlement acceptable to the Complainant and reasonable to the Commission, is achieved;

   (d) The Complainant is kept fully informed of the progress of the complaints investigation;

   (e) The result of the Commission's investigation and any recommendations are reported (in accordance with the guidance to be found at paragraph 9 on page 7 and para 24 page 16) to both the Complainant and those complained about; and

   (f) The Commission monitors the exercise of its complaints remit and in particular the achievement of the objectives set out above.

3. **Terminology**

   A complaint for the purpose of this procedure is any communication received by the Commission or any Commissioner which;

   (a) falls within the Commission complaints remit as set out in Section 120(1)(b) of the Act; and

   (b) In the case of such communications received by Commissioners while visiting hospitals or mental nursing homes cannot be satisfactorily resolved during the visit and require action to be taken after the conclusion of the visit.

   The definition includes complaints which merit investigation but cannot be investigated because the patient does not give or withdraws consent.

4. **Time limits**

   The following time limits should apply to Commission complaints investigations:

   (a) All complaints received in writing *will* be acknowledged in writing within two working days of receipt.

   (b) A more detailed response should be provided within three weeks of receipt of a Commission complaint. If this is not possible then an appropriate holding letter should be sent within that time;

   (c) The investigation of most Commission complaints should be concluded within fourteen weeks. Where circumstances prevent the achievement of this objective, then the complainant should be informed and then kept further informed at not more than three weekly intervals; and

   (d) Where the investigation of a Commission complaint is not concluded within twenty weeks of receipt of the complaint, then the matter should be referred to the Chief Executive for review.

In order to ensure that the investigation of complaints is carried out as promptly as possible, the time limits referred to above should be adhered to in as many investigations as possible. It is important, however, to ensure that compliance with the time limits is not to the detriment of the quality of the investigation. Where it is necessary to take longer than the time limits allow for, it is *essential* to keep the complainant informed.

APPENDIX 6

COMPLAINT AGAINST COMMISSIONERS:
POLICY AND PROCEDURE

Policy and Procedure

This document sets out a policy and procedure for the Commission to follow when complaints against Commissioners are received from complainants apart from other Commissioners or Commission staff.

The Commission is a Health Authority and therefore, the provisions of the Hospital Complaints Procedures Act 1985 apply.

1. **The Policy**

   (a) **Preface**

   All complaints to which this Policy and Procedure applies will be considered seriously and promptly and investigated thoroughly and fairly. All complaints are potentially valuable indicators of the Commissions performance and provide pointers by which the Commissions quality of service can be measured.

   (b) **Objectives**

   The objective of this policy is reconciliation on the basis of established facts. In the event that this is not possible, then the vice Chairman (in Stage I) or the Chairman (in Stage II) will make a finding. (See below).

   (c) **Time limits**

   Save in exceptional circumstances all complaints investigation under this policy should be completed within six weeks of receipt of the complaint.

3. **Designated Officer**

   The Chief Executive is the Commissions 'designated Officer' to whom all complaints to which this policy refers will be referred. He will be responsible for ensuring that the Commissions policy and procedure is implemented in relation to each complaint received.

   In stage I (see below) of the procedure the Vice Chairman of the Commission will be informed of the progress of any complaints investigations and it will be the Vice Chairman and not the designated Officer who will make any provisional finding as to whether a complaint is justified. In stage II of the procedure it will be the Chairman who will (where necessary) make a finding as to whether a complaint is justified.

4. **The procedure**

   Stage I

   (a) **Receipt and initial action**

   All complaints received will be acknowledged by return and a copy of the complaints policy and procedure will be sent to the Complainant. All complaints will be allocated a complaints against Commissioner number.

   Where a complaint is received in writing, a copy of it will be sent immediately to the Commissioner/s concerned for their comments.

   Where a complaint is made verbally a transcript of the complaint will be sent immediately to:

       i. the Complainant to check for accuracy;

       ii. the Commissioner concerned for their comments.

   Where necessary the designated Officer (in consultation with the Vice Chairman) will seek further information.

   (b) **Action after enquiries made**

       i. **Complaints report**

       Once the designated Officer has received all the information referred to above, he will prepare a complaints report identifying any aspects of the complaint which are the subject of disagreement between the Complainant and the Commissioner concerned. On completion the designated Officer will refer this to the Vice Chairman;

ii. on receipt the Vice Chairman will decide if any further enquiries are necessary *and* if a meeting between the Complainant and the Commission/s concerned is necessary to clarify any unresolved matters or to seek a resolution.

At this stage the Vice Chairman will also offer a meeting to the Commissioner/s complained about.

iii. Once (ii) above is completed, then the Vice Chairman will further consider the matter and make a decision as to:

a. whether the matter has been resolved and if so what action should be taken; or

b. In the absence of resolution whether the complaint is justified and what action should be taken. Such a finding will be a *provisional finding*.

Where the Vice Chairman makes a provisional finding that the complaint is justified, then both the Complainant and the Commissioner/s concerned will be notified immediately about the finding together with (in broad outline) the reasons supporting the finding. Both complainant and Commissioner will be advised that if they are dissatisfied with the finding, then they may request that the matter be referred to *Stage II*.

Stage II

(a) Where the Complainant or Commissioner complained against disagrees with the provisional finding made by the Vice Chairman, then they should notify the designated Officer. On receipt of such notification the designated Officer will be to refer the matter to the Chairman, who will:

i. where necessary call on a designated Officer to seek further information; and/or

ii. recommend a further meeting between the complainant and the Commissioners concerned. In order to clarify any misunderstandings, disputed facts or to seek a resolution of the matter.

(b) Where it is not possible to resolve the matter, the Chairman will then make a *finding* as to whether the complaint is justified and what action (if necessary) needs to be taken.

APPENDIX 7

WITH-HOLDING OF MAIL AND COMMISSION REVIEW POWERS POLICY AND PROCEDURE

A) Introduction

The powers of hospital managers to examine and with-hold postal packets and their duties when they exercise those powers, are set out in Section 134 of the Mental Health Act 1983 and the Mental Health (Hospital, Guardianship and Consent to Treatment) Regulations (S.1 1983 No. 893). Where a packet or anything contained in it is with-held the duties include one to notify within seven days, the patient and, if known, the person by whom the packet was sent, of a right of review of the decision by the Mental Health Act Commission.

By Section 121(7) and (8) of the Act and the regulations, the Commission is given complete discretion in the way it should conduct this review (which must be made to it within six months of the receipt of the notice) and it may direct that the packet be not with-held.

B) Procedures for the exercise of the Commission's powers:

1) Relevant CVT/SHP Executive Officer or visiting Commissioner receive "appeal" from patient and/or sender of package. This need not necessarily be in writing.

2) A minimum of two, and not more than three Commissioners nominated by CVT/SHP convenor to review decision.

3) Relevant Executive Officer notifies hospital of receipt of "appeal" and of the arrangements made by Commissioners to hear it, and asks for their written explanation of the grounds for with-holding the package or item within the terms of Section 134(1) and (2) and the details of the procedure they have followed.

4) A visit should be arranged at which the following action should be taken.
    (a) If patient is appellant, Commissioners interview as on complaints visit.
    (b) If sender is appellant, Commissioners decide whether to invite him to be present or if written submission will suffice.
    (c) Comissioners should examine hospital's procedural documents to satisfy themselves that the requirements of the Act have been followed.
    (d) Commissioners to examine documents, article etc., with-held.
    (e) Commissioners, at their discretion, to interview all staff who had any direct influence on the particular decision to with-hold.
    (f) Commissioners to interview the person appointed by the managers, who has with-held the package or item, especially if considering over-riding the decision.

(N.B: If appropriate and parties agree Commissioners could interview appellant and parties (e) and (f) together).

5) Commissioners make decision and notify appellant(s) and managers in writing. If the Commissioners think it is desirable, and especially if the patient is mentally impaired, they may also tell the patient orally.

6) Commissioners consider whether cases raises any issues which should be reported to SHP/CVT team meeting, relevant NSC meeting or CPC.

C) Notification to Hospitals

CPC agreed that when the policy has been approved each special hospital should be advised.

APPENDIX 8

POLICY ON RACE

Introduction

The Race Relations Act 1976 defines two kinds of racial discrimination:

Direct discrimination arises where a person treats another person less favourably on racial grounds than he treats, or would treat, someone else. "Racial grounds" means any of the following grounds: colour, race, nationality (including citizenship) or ethnic or national origins.

Indirect discrimination consists of treatment which may be described as equal in a formal sense as between different racial groups but discriminatory in its effect on one particular group. A 'racial group' is one defined by reference to one or more of the following: colour, race, nationality (including citizenship) or ethnic or national origins.

In upholding Race Relations legislation applicable to the whole of Great Britain, the Mental Health Act Commission is committed to the following aims and actions.

Aims

1.1 To ensure equality of opportunity to all members and staff of the Commission to participate in the organisation and work of the Commission irrespective of race, colour, culture or nationality.

1.2 To ensure that detained patients and others dealt with by the Commission are treated equally, irrespective of race etc. (as above).

1.3 To ensure that Health Authorities, Social Services Departments and other agencies concerned with the treatment/care of detained patients deliver such treatment/care equally, irrespective of race etc. (as above).

Actions

2.1 **Confronting Racism**

2.1 The Commission will take positive action to:

Prevent and counteract the effects of discriminatory practice on racial grounds by any member of the Commission, its staff or anyone acting on behalf of the Commission.

To ensure that issues concerning racial and cultural matters will not be 'marginalised'; such 'marginalisation' will be construed as 'indirect discrimination' and treated as such under this policy.

2.2 **Training**

For those who have not already undertaken similar training, the Commission will provide training for its members and staff in:

The personal awareness of racism, the recognition of racist practices and behaviour, and the ways in which racism may be counteracted within the Commission.

The recognition and ways of counteracting racism within Health Authorities, Departments of Social Services and other agencies concerned with the treatment/care of detained patients.

2.3 **Work of Commission**

2.3.1 The Commission will ensure that its policies, procedures and activities are free of discriminatory practices on racial grounds.

2.3.2 The Commission will endeavour to ensure that policies, procedures and activities of Health Authorities and Social Service Departments are free of discriminatory practices on racial grounds.

2.4 **Members of the Commission**

The Commission will ensure that all its members are involved in the work of the Commission according to their knowledge and experience, taking note of any special knowledge they may have through personal experience of racial and cultural issues; no member will be excluded from any of the Commission's activities on the grounds of race.

2.5 **Advice on Race Relations and Monitoring**

The Commission will instruct its Standing Committee on Race and Culture to:

1. To study and report on issues of race and culture as they relate to the Commission's work.

2. To advise the CPC and the Commission on relevant issues and to contribute to the promotion of a greater understanding within the Commission of matters relevant to race and culture and the development of Commission policies, procedures and practice that reflects that understanding.

3. To monitor the implementation of any policy promulgated by and for the Commission and to make proposals for updating where necessary.

4. To prepare material for the Biennial Report.

5. To undertake other relevant tasks as referred to it by the Commission, CPC or the Chief Executive.

Publications used for reference

Home Office and the Central Office of Information (1977) *Racial Discrimination. A Guide to the Race Relations Act 1976*, HMSO, London.

Kalsi, Nirveen and Constantinides, Pamela (1989) *Working towards Racial Equality in Health Care. The Haringey Experience*, Kings Fund Centre, London.

King's Fund Equal Opportunities Task Force (1989) *Health Authority Equal Opportunities Committees*, King's Fund Publishing Office, London.

Mind Policy Paper 2 (1986) *Mental Health Services in a Multi-Racial Society*, MIND Publications, London.

Background reading

Britain, A and Maynard, M (1984) *Sexism, Racism and Oppression*, Blackwell, Oxford.

Fernando, Suman (1989) *Race and Culture in Psychiatry*, Tavistock/Routledge, London.

Husband, Charles (ed.) (1982) *'Race' in Britain*, Hutchinson, London.

Kovel, Joel (1988) *White Racism. A Psychohistory*, Free Association Books, London.

Sartre, Jean-Paul (1948) *Anti-Semite and Jew*, Translated by G J Becker, Schocken Books, New York.

Approved by the Central Policy Committee on 1 February 1990